BRAVE

FOR THE UNCLAIMED PEOPLE

LORE DE ANGELES

BRAVE | FOR THE UNCLAIMED PEOPLE

First published in Australia by LOTHBROKSIGURD, 2021
This paperback edition published by LOTHBROKSIGURD, 2021
Copyright © Lore de Angeles, 2021

All rights reserved. No reproduction, copy or transmission of this publication may be made without written permission. No paragraph of this publication may be reproduced, copied or transmitted save with written permission or in accordance with the provisions of the Copyright Act 1956 (as amended). Any person who does any unauthorized act in relation to this publication may be liable to criminal prosecution and civil claims for damages. Including Internet usage, without written permission from the author except in the case of brief quotations embodied in critical articles and reviews.

ISBN 978-0-64857545-3-8
Australia/Pacifica 2021
Cover photography Serenity de Angeles
Cover design Zo Damage zodamage.com/
Production LOTHBROKSIGURD, Australia

BRAVE

Brave is not something a person feels.
Neither is courage.
Neither is fearlessness.

The above are observations from the outside.
Inside is usually terror.
Adrenalin.

An action necessary when there is no other choice.

...

DE ANGELES' OTHER BOOKS

1987   The Way of the Goddess, England
1990   The Way of Merlyn, England
2000   Witchcraft Theory and Practice, A Wiccan 101 Approach
2002   When I See the Wild God, Urban Celtic Witchcraft
2004   Pagan Visions for a Sustainable Future, Essays
2005   The Quickening, 1st in the Traveler Series, Magical Realism
2006   The Shining Isle, 2nd in the Traveler Series, Magical Realism
2007   Tarot, Theory and Practice
2012   Magdalene | The Witch of the Grail Legends
2013   The Feast of Flesh and Spirit
2015   Priteni, the Decimation of the Indigenous Britons
2016   Initiation | A Memoir
2017   The Skellig, A Shapechanger Tale
2018   Witch | For Those Who Are
2019   Under Snow, 3rd in the Traveler Series, Magical Realism
2020   Advanced Tarot | The Voyage of Prophecy

Please note that the words *witch, druid, draoí, draíochta, beansídhe, seelie, sorcerer, gentry* and *storyteller* are interchangeable throughout this work. They're the same thing. I simply pull, moreso, on a Celtic/Gaelic and common terminology to hopefully alleviate presumptions.

ACKNOWLEDGMENTS

Katrina Grace Kelly, of *Cribmates and Adoption Reversal Australia*[1], held me up when I was ready to break. You took me all the way to the Supreme Court and calmly aided me to win, so what do I say? I am a free person, today, because of you. Guts and glory, Grace—guts and glory. Thank you.

Margaret Watson, Tricia Dearden and others at PARC[2] who worked with me, out of sheer kindness, for 20 years, you found me a mother. Peter O'Brien. You found me a father.

Mother: Glad Shirley Green (died 2013)
Father: Eduard J Manso (Visconte) de Villa (died 2016)

A SPECIAL DEDICATION

In memory of all who couldn't wait and took their own lives.

To all the women shamed and bewildered.

None of this was our fault.

...

---

[1] https://www.facebook.com/AdopteeRightsAU/posts/adoption-reversal-our-email-address-any-australian-adoptees-who-want-their-adopt/317467448915114/
[2] https://www.benevolent.org.au/services-and-programs/list-of-programs/post-adoption-resource-centre-nsw

CONTENTS

1	Cave of a Bewildered Mammoth	15
2	Introduction—Them Ol Dark Piney Woods	19
3	Faerie in the Alley	21
4	How to Break Rules	29
5	Bear Dreaming	35
6	Take the Darkened Road	39
7	Stories to Crack the Tarmac	41
8	Crowhearted	43
9	The Name of the World is Alive	47
10	Singing Concrete from Sleep	55
11	Did Some Fool Say Follow Your Dreams?	57
12	Hush Li'l Baby	59
13	Uppity White Woman	61
14	Never a God	69
15	Bone Magic	71
16	You Can Hear the Freedom	73
17	Dread Amongst the Roots	83
18	The Hunter, I	95
19	A Tad of Rapture	105
20	Roadkill in a Once-Upon-a-Time Forest	109
21	Timelessness (An Interview)	123
22	Descending the Bone Scaffold	127
23	On Being Anonymous and Lost	137
24	Bone Woman	141
25	The Guilt Delusion	147
26	The Language of Animacy	153
27	Broken Tongue	155
28	Being Real in an Age of Duplicity	159
29	Razor Wire Blues	163
30	Drowned	167
31	Witchin in the Wildwood	171
32	Color Me Grey	175
33	One Woman, Ten Men	187
34	Don't Cause an Earthquake	201
35	Feral—Rewilding Language	209

36	The Devil is Real, and It's on the 6 O'clock News	219
37	Fragile	229
38	Changeling	233
39	That Other Witchcraft	237
40	Of Mice, Martial Arts and Vaginas	241
41	Wolves in Cages	251
42	Brave	253
43	Won't Never be Me	271
44	Kingmaker	273
45	The Song of Levington Blade	275
46	Mutha	281
47	Woman Mountain	283
48	Suggested Reading	285
49	End Notes	287
50	About Lore de Angeles	289

CAVE OF A BEWILDERED MAMMOTH

A note on the use—or lack thereof—of capitalization

> *We accept with nary a thought that the names of people are capitalized. To write "george washington" would be to strip the man of his special status as a human. It would be laughable to write "Mosquito" if it were in reference to a flying insect, but acceptable if we were discussing a brand of boat. Capitalization conveys a certain distinction, the elevated position of humans and their creations in the hierarchy of beings.*
>
> —Robin Wall Kimmerer, *Braiding Sweetgrass,* 2020

Having digested the above, after reading *Braiding Sweetgrass* from now-ratty cover to cover, I concur. As such, some of this work could seem confusing. I am utterly lacking in apology because I trust, after all the years of writing... you. I trust you. Sometimes I capitalize, others, I don't. Random? So bury me.

This book is to honor those who are lost, in hiding or who choose to disappear. Those of our heritage, as a Celtic People (albeit, some of us in exile from the hills and valleys and rivers and caves that call us, ceaseless as tide), stolen. You are correct. We may not have our language, but pride, and stories old and new, sustain us during these wandering years; these lost generations.

Music, culture and hunting, art, community, initiations, markings and clothing have altered but we are still here. Enlivened, different and considered, are the new-old gifts we have to share with other indigenous peoples.

To do less, or concede a forgottenness, is impossible.

...

Within the dance of death's embrace
the seed is carried past the veil.
It is unfolding to its pattern
and a forest is its grail...

INTRODUCTION

THEM OL' DARK PINEY WOODS

You just keep starin outa that window, hear? An don't you heed that teacher over there. It's all repetition, darlin. Time to make fresh tracks off the asphalt, off the concrete, off the how-to. Into the older, life-affirming ways. Weavin an plantin seeds, an raftin up, against a current most times, to the source of the river. An knowin what's gonna live when you are dead. When *we* are dead.

Nobody can tell me not to drop g's anymore. They now all older'n me. All to dust. Their silly textbooks didn't feed em, now, did they?

No point havin a brain less you think for yourself.

...

FAERIE IN THE ALLEY

EARTH

Sitka spruce! The seed must have blown in from the great plantation across the mountains. They were, as far as I could tell, the only trees on the reserve. They were, as far as I could tell, the only trees on the reserve, except for those clinging to the inaccessible slopes of the ravine. The white plague—or so I thought at the time—had destroyed the rest.

—George Monbiot, *Feral*

Before the roman infantry invades mountains and fertile valleys and shoreline habitats, I am here. I am *Brigant*, and the human *Brigant* children are sometimes called *carvette*—the *People of the Deer*. Current positioning, on a nautical map, is latitude: 54° 29' 59.99" n, longitude: -3° 14' 60.00" w.

I am Cumbria, and although this is difficult to define, I will say that I am cousin to rivers, lochs and aft-shot off the western isles. I am the waters of what is called the Solway Firth, just north of Carlisle, that bring us the stories of *smelt*, flap-footed seals, basking *siarcs*, blue mussels and curlew; mona—Ynis Môn—is known in a modern, shallow, *know-little-profess-much-dialect*, as Anglesey or, perhaps, the Isle of Man that *tacitus*, buddy to the bitter politician *claudius*, writes of as a land of druids. I am standing stones and the first forests of oak and rowan, pine, blackwood, birch, spruce and grave-dappling yew.

And let's not forget the wee islands—named by the Norse—of Walney, Fowdray (*piel*), Roa and Foulney, all *laimrig*-safe, for anchorage, amidst the terror of a *beum-sléibhe* from the west, on trade route currents, puffing out the mainsl's of the big ships and the bobbing insanity of coracle and curragh, by ocean route twixt Éire, Breize (Brittany) and, well, all lands traversable throughout the epoch known as the bronze age. Lands once also called *Rheged*.

Have I been fought over? Yes. Am I extant? Well, one woman is still here. One man. The children are here (or else otherwhere, by way of fate or tragedy). These grandchildren are living also, so how can I *not* be present, wherever governments, traders, invaders and deeply entrenched trauma have driven us? Despite over fifteen thousand oceanic miles between some arcane, vast, unpredictable Dreamtime island, beneath the wide dark skies of *Koodjal Djooka* and me, this ancestral home.

DROWNER WATER

The spirit who bideth by himself In the land of mist and snow, He loved the bird that loved the man Who shot him with his bow.

—T.S. Coleridge, *The Ryme of the Ancient Mariner*

I am *keld* and *fen*. Reed-singing marshland, and I am home to teal, and the Alban grandeur of the little egret, oyster catchers, barnacle geese; the eerie, seelie language—*weerloo*—of a night-calling curlew. Hence I am bogs and territories of peat, primordial, drowned plant-people cousins, once vast beyond comprehension, gracing earth from some glacial estimate of twelve thousand years deep. The end of a mythic and legendary ice age, or two. Or three. Or whatever.

I am Eden, river of the *black fell moss*, cousin of *swale*, and *isurā*, and the journey of salmon kin from spawn to demise. Dawn is high in the *wild boar fell*, and night is Carlyle, 1,824 feet above the shores of our sister lands. I flow east, then north, receiving chat and fealty from the many *becks* that join me from along the vast mountain chain known, by some, as the Pennines. We skirt the verdancy of a forest whose true name is lost in the dead mouths of ancestors, stolen by the english to now be called *Inglewood*, in the eleven hundreds.

I *froth* and *blinter*, viridescent and storm-tossed, winter-dark and cloud-filled, past *Long Meg and her Daughters*, to eventually reunite with the sea, amidst the *rime* and *bar'ber*—the *pirr* – all around me. Beneath the lights of *An Réalta Thuaidh*, tossing a million years of *clitter*, *gritstone* and *tuff*, to and fro along ancient shores and estuaries that summon smugglers and survivors. Soothed by arctic freeze sometimes, sometimes doomed by *hob-gob*, often an *endragoned* danger, seldom by calm or fancy.

I am *baari* river-stone-carved veins, brooks and burns coursing from Solway Firth in the west, to the Firth of Forth, here, choking a bit on the abandoned shopping trolleys, condoms, little orange-tipped syringes, cigarette butts, discarded slushy cups and occasionally, but regularly, the body parts of some bloated, drug-fucked, forgotten, abandoned, mutilated and murdered dead. Dùn Èideann (Edinburgh), that grand fortress made of grandfather stone, now leaning towards me calling, *Take me, take me now*! On this epic excursion from the Irish Sea to the *shock*, and *whale-mother-depths* that human people call *Muir Lochlainn*, far to the north where the *finnock* swim.

I am heard, but not always seen (by the human eye), in the *grimlins*.

CLOUDY STARRY SKY

Oh, we are hard to kill. Four thousand years into the long ago is the *when* attributed to the when of our *under-earth-ness* story but... what about now? Who are those who write about *dúthchas* (this writer's human children) when most have forgotten the legends of ancestral *treedom*? Of the hunter and the hunted?

Yet we are dead. Are we? Or so it is written. So. I am confused, and I am confounded because beneath this mighty soil, within the secrets of the mountains and the magic and the mystery of the Northern Lights I am majestic still; enchanted, even, of the sídhe and the nurseries of the *cladd*. Within the *weem*, I nightmare, although awake. Roots engorged with life, beneath peat, the heather, the *roarie-bummlers*, still with sap a-plenty, and ready for man-looking forgetfulness. Waiting until... a thousand, thousand *Svalbard Globale Frøhvelv* barrows, of the Arctic human-person kind, that nurture unborn forests and foraging memories, awakens, in some momentarily unrealized epoch, to the bull-moose trumpet or the wolf-pack howl. In another day, in another century, when liberated (oh, that incessant fear of starvation, of a poverty that forests never cause) by that not-forgotten piping of eagle-bone flute, or scream of protest by sister vixen.

For Mother Earth to give birth she needs relax her bothered and relentless rain, release the dormant to be living, instead.

We say, *I remember you*! as we cut the last lamb's throat, kindly, holdingly, remembering that once a forest, always a forest, given just enough breathing room to seek the Sky, no matter that the air is filled with the detritus of cotton factories and coal mines, and families driven to despair through the greed of some stranger in a bureaucracy somewhere, cloistered and bland, a fact hidden by the façade of whiskey and cocaine; to the violation and carelessness of the clans by thanes, headline-grabbing prime ministers and media, not understanding (or on pretence of ignorance) the rightness of deep-veined ancestry, as though a paper decree holds more weight than a dolmen, a murder of ravens or an ancestral kinship system. Remembered. Long before there were scratches on a page trapping words into idioms, metaphors of self-glory and self-aggrandizing propaganda.

FIRE IN THE HEAD

These wings are the beauty of the poet's soul. The songs, thus flying immortal from their mortal parent, are pursued by clamorous flights of censures, which swarm in far greater numbers, and threaten to devour them; but these last are not winged. At the end of a very short leap they fall plump down, and rot, having received from the souls out of which they came no beautiful wings. But the melodies of the poet ascend, and leap, and pierce into the deeps of infinite time.

—Ralph Waldo Emerson, *The Poet*

And now I feel the need to sleep for a million years.

A human being, or so, might read this and think, *What do you matter? What does it matter that you are what you are*? And I am confounded that *you* is not *I*, or even *we*. As though, at some crossroads, people stopped singing and meeting. Stopped remembering. Forswore knowing us as family. The grief I experience at having these children's backs turned away from this love is devastating. This tenderness of kin, lost. This memory of elder orality seemingly vanquished.

Well, Voldemort, upstart of faux-wizardry that you hide behind, with your Apple *smart* watch and your *louis vuitton* running shoes, you cannot set your bedding down, up here. This *scarped* soul. This *moss-breek*. You will not be *lound* from me. No *imlioc*, no *glisk*, no *fardon* and no *ystafell* in which you can hide. That you choose to call a passage to within the earth—and a place of secrets where only they and I can hear and know—a grave (where, in truth, no ancestor ever was buried) shows only that you believe some resurrection fiction, and not the spirals of birth and death that is that of seed, stem, leaf, bud, flower, fruit. That you call worship, where there is no god but *us*, and *I*, and *we*.

What happens if *you* forget? If *you* are forgotten? Is there a reason for the idea of death? Are you so lonely you can't understand our language? Our *zwer*? Don't you remember we are *knowe*? That we are *daal'mist*? Lighty-dark? *Geal-cauld* and the *plutsh* of walking boots hollow-ringing in the haunted, hushed, torchlit barrows of ancestors, singing of *Merlin of the Borders*, and mother mackerel and *Morgan le Fey*? Children's stories hiding a deeper wisdom. Just in case.

I am not forgotten, *carvette*; not so drookit I can't feel the sun or raise a voice in *sheepy-silver* shine at all. I am no ink-drawn border on google maps: no England. No Scotland, Wales, Skye, Man, Ireland, Lewis, Harris, Mór, Ratharsair, Orkney, Scilly or Stornoway. These are names that are written to push me—us—from our insides. As if we could. *I am*, that's enough to say *we are*.

I AM FEY AND THAT IS BIRTHRIGHT

As if the idea of glittery, painted, winged, diminutive inventions of an invader species could diminish us. Call us "fairies" as though *we* are not *I*, as though *I* am not the whole land, the entire sky, the everywhere who is river and underworld cavern. Could warp us into a bit of no importance when, in fact *I* am, *we* are, gentry. We are the *good folk*. I am sídhe, and William Wallace, Robert the Bruce and Sterling. Calgacus and Culloden, Annie Lennox, the Monarch of the Glen and oh—once—Elephants with long straight tusks. Black bears who were all killed off to make silly hats for some *inntrenger*-appointed *king*, or *queen* (such pompous titling words, as though one person has more importance than another). I am carboniferous limestone formed about, oh, 340 million years gone. I am Pendle Hill. Sandstone and shale and *gritstone* moorlands. I am *drumlins*, yes, and I am Bronte and Connery and Connolly. I am cousin to the *dyke swarm* off the Isle of Mull, 56.4392° n 6.0009° w, off the dark peaty coast of Alba. I am the ill-fated, possible vilified in some propaganda-driven, first century media condemnation: Cartimandua.

History is an opinion with an agenda. Its curse is that it is a story written, not spoken, that of men, of what is taken and who is harmed and who is better than everyone slaughtered, no matter the kindred species, no matter that the land burns because of it. History uses words as though they are *flosh* instead of a *winterbourne*, in the wonder and bafflement, and laughter and *tripple* of us.

I am, we are, here is...

DIVULGENCE

World.

I was body-born as who I am now, on a long-occupied but violently invaded island that got called—eventually—Australia. I was the firstborn and the only born human child of Arctic *ness* that salmon-leaps as far back as records are kept. Parents forgotten. Here for just a generation. Dead in some high-walled graveyard, or else ashes that are nourishment for controlled roses, with a hint of *christianness* to dishonor the fire in their blood.

Have I a right to be here? In this landscape? This person-land of ancient differences and extremes? Long-befossilled desert and Uluru stone? No. I have never been offered permission. Not by the First Nation human people, not by Emu people, not by a wedgetail Eagle-person or Barramundi clan. I am the people of so many Norther-Lights-people-countries I forget, just for a moment, how many.

Until Great White Shark, Goanna, Eastern Brown Snake, the jumping jack Ant colony, red dust, oceanic rip and giant old growth mountain

Ash say, *Here, here, be here and sing to us of unknown or unremembered being, since Gondwana, child of soil and sun and star...* I remain a changeling from the *seelie court*, left in a place in which I

should not, really, thrive. For that I apologize with the whole of us.

    NOW

I bring stories. I *will* offer them. That's what I have, it's who I am. Who *we* are. But who we are is where we belong. And what, of that, can we bring to the gathering? Whether we tell of *loch* or *ffrwd*, of decimation or invasion.

Better that, than to merely say, *Hi, my name is Jim and I'm in IT...*

    as though that is all.

        ....as though that is all...

    ...

HOW TO BREAK RULES

IN THE FIRST PLACE

When we're children we get told what to wear. There are rules for little boys. There are rules for little girls. Rules exist to keep us safe, don't they? We're ruled by the folk in suits and mummy-clothes. Occasionally by those in fashionable frocks and subdued jewelry. Refined people, of good stock. Middle management. Money. The suburb. Particularly, though, by the color of one's pelt.

Us human-people animals be ruled by the ones with dicks and pale pelts: skin. If there was a ladder, upright against the side of a windowless, concrete building, untagged, un-grafitti'd, conforming—in every sense of the word—to the rules of remaining upright and immoveable, those folks be on the top rung with cattle prods and serious expressions and no piercings. Sometimes with a crate of kalashnikovs or lead-tipped whips. Or a religious book and a media presence. Rules are meant to force us to forget. Love, belonging, individuality, art, courage, equality.

I've thought about this. Sat on the couch on the front porch, late at night, eyes blurred with streetlight, horizontal rain and the violent, fragmented red blink of the security system protecting the house across the street from invaders. And I came to a conclusion...

MAKE EM IF YOU BREAK EM

First, I made a mental list of all the rules been set up since I was young. Wearing a uniform to school, being threatened to stand in line. Knowing when to raise a hand and when it was safer to shut up. The rules of what being pretty were. Rules about what being a girl meant; what being a boy meant. Rules about spelling and how to speak. We had rules once, that said we had to stand, in assembly, and sing *"god save the queen"*. Rules that required us to *not* get our ears pierced (it was called *common*, as though that is an unpleasant thing and not free-to-roam forest; people deriding European immigrants as *wogs* and *dagos*). To not have sex indiscriminately—with or without a condom—and even if indiscriminately, to do so with the deceitfully disnified idea that something wonderful could possibly come from sharing such intimacy. Like love. Because it won't. Like companionship. Like joy. No. Entrenched rules demanded that if we had a vagina, we were not supposed to play with it in public. If we had a dick we could, but, to the dismay of the young nowadays (officially, according to sanctioned church and state, only with people with vaginas.

We even had—or have—rules that intimidate us by demanding *you can't do that, don't you dare do that, if you do that, don't do that* ... the rule being not to ask *why*. That's because rules also exist that say you have to respect your elders. Your *betters*. Whether they're zoned out on the couch watching daytime TV, off their faces on oxycontin, bashing each other with the jagged bit of what was a bottle, making jokes, around the barbie on a sunday afternoon, about tits or blacks, or trans, or q-anon or who should win the cricket and that the Indian team cheated, they had to have didn't they? If they're in the media spotlight, running Rio Tinto, getting away with raping little choir boys or committing genocide because of some religion or other. That's in
the rule book, isn't it?

HERITAGE

So, I thought I'd write a recipe for the next generation, because I've done as much as I can to break those that seem set in polyurethane—for now—without actually going to gaol or being, otherwise, institutionalized... Oh wait; that second one happened already. Long time ago now. Dodged a bullet there for a few years since, eh? Broke the rules, monumentally, in the years of an anarchist, heretical, artistically-poxed, perennially and belligerently opinionated youth.
So...
1. Know the rules. That doesn't sound like what is necessary, but it is because one has to be creative. So...
2. Know the rules. Then:

KNOW WHY

3. Know *why* you want to break the rules. What is it about said rules that piss you off? Always handy to write that down. Keep a list. Cite your sources. It helps when you get to the place where you need to defend yourself. And you will, at first.

KNOW WHAT

4. Know *what* to replace the extant rules of anything with. If you've got nothing, then the outcome is assuredly, also, nothing:
    a. There's so much rubbish around *hypothetically* breaking rules. This insult can be like stagnant water in a pond of plastic and old Maccas containers; a pond that was once a river, and will be again if we just listen *to* the river and not the people-animals that are fucking it up. Because adding more garbage to the pond, without even knowing it was once a river, is just stupid. And you'll end up in an old people's home sucking your steak through a straw,

wondering where everyone who agreed with you once, or who you once agreed with, have gone.
   b. Because lots of people who try to break the existing rules get smashed with water cannon, or herded up and sent to a re-education camp where they get to sing songs about *jesus*, or the flag, or getting turned straight or… the rules.
   c. You could end up lonely anyway so…

KNOW HOW

5. Here's the interesting part. You have to know enough… by goom, you *really* have to know enough of *how* the rules work, to be able to replace them. And that's the glitch. You do. Have to replace them. With your own. Aristotle's *horror vacui* (re-termed *natura abhorret vacuum* by Rabelais in the 16th-century) a priori in this case. Perhaps in all cases. I'm not sure if it's a rule or merely an opinion without a basis.

If you're clear, if you've double-challenged your honest (or biased) agendas, who'll get hurt, how far you're prepared to go, to know when art becomes caricature, when divergence becomes just an excuse to be a brat, when there's really no point.

If you're clear then you won't have this rule-challenge/change kill you, endanger the village or the herd, backfire to the point where you can hardly breath with anger, then yes. Do it. But cleverly. Those people-animals on the top rung want you to fail and come across as a fool. To point out that you haven't really got roots to your rules.

DEEP ROOTS

6. I'm not suggesting that you *only* study, but I am suggesting you do. History for the propaganda, social sciences for the propaganda, religion for… well…

If not study, then apprentice to an expert. If I want the greatest saddle, I better know how to make the one that's the best already. And why I want to change what is considered the best.

Research. If you're going to claim ancestors from a particular tribal culture or confederacy, well, don't make it up, okay? That's just plain rude. It's self-indulgent. It denigrates the people you want to be like. Everything about it is vulgar and blatant bigotry. It's *so john-wayne-kills-the-Indians*, so *margaret court*. It's a copout and it puts you, me, any one of us pale people in the skip marked *privileged colonizers and tryhards who wanna be Indigenous-X*. What do you want? What's your motive? Laziness is the reason, I got that. You got that?

7. Don't lie.
8. Do lie, if it means your kids are safe by you doing so.
9. If you went through the fun part of conceiving, and you get to experience the peculiar enchantment of the outcome of birthing a future generational human-animal, you have to be real. Or they're going to smash the fuck out of your lies when they are old enough. Which is probably about nine. It's about then they realize you're a person, and that any idea you were/are a god is flushed down the toilet.

In addition to challenges of power, we also need to continue to develop and experiment with successful ways to organize as united people in ways that address, challenge, and transcend divisions of race, class, gender, ability, sexuality, citizenship and unequal structural power.

—Chris Crass, *On Social Justice.*

10. Be consistent.
11. Learn language. We are so conned by rhetoric and outdated, bigoted metaphor that it can almost negate what anyone says.

EXAMPLE

I sat ruminating, with a new friend—a psychotherapist—over tea, and we were discussing body language; how 80% of what we comprehend is wordless; is from the way another person stands, or what we physically experience.

I said, *Like fear. I experience it in the gut.*
They said, *Oh, you mean the solar plexus chakra*!

Two things: First, I admit, the person did not really know me. This was the first time we had spoken at any length. Second, they were, therefore, unaware of why I sat like I did, like a person who just smashed their head on the corner of the overhead cupboard, with probably a small dribble escaping from chin to throat as I fought to not say anything. But the me of me, nah, couldn't do it.

Me: *You speak Latin and Sanskrit*!
Them: *What*?
Me: *You just corrected me.*

BREAK RULES, MAKE RULES

1. Remove the ladder.
2. Build a place not made of concrete.
3. Be prepared for it to have windows.
4. Let yourself live and die by your own rules.
5. Walk tall.
6. Be real.
7. Have a sense of humor or people will think you're painful and nothing will be accomplished. Ergo: also, be compassionate.
8. Listen.

...

BEAR DREAMING

That fen, yes. The tomb where the lynx dreams
Of wild green eyes and once unwounded water

Where a bear drank deep above the river yearning
For later snow, just in case, and cubs at the breast, all sleeping.
I have not sailed away to a new-old land

But hunt, I really do, as spirit-haunted fog and daylight soft
deliverance, among the rain-wet rook heights,
and I dream that I remember; that I am not lost…

Crags above the slag heap looking—looming—like old clergy,
Down upon me, clean, buried in memory. I yearn and rage, and I
know that I am your wildness, and not also your sickness, or their
sheep or that pick or chainsaw-grinding violation. Stone hungry,
For what we are, for who we are, and the winding,
Rambling wolf-howl of us, deep
Within the spruce forest. I do!
I remember because I am you.
The pain of thighs that are wounded by ivy and nettle's children,
twined
With holly-red berry and kelp-snarl. And I am scabby with the

Wind's snap, the peak above the cliff that keeps
Watch, out on the harbor, for mother Orca,
In the sleet-scoured, oyster-old
Deep dark ancestral blue

Remembering, for all the dead who flood this blood with living red…
Selkies heads above the ebb, all huge eyes and silence,
Stalking, as though they are predators, as though the black lung didn't break me,

And all the fathers who bowed their backs, but not their eyes, to a whip or a banishment

Leaving me to cleave the messages, to that otter-lover in the sun-remembered gorse, gleaning meaning from the cloud we thought one day would lift us up to heaven
Before we learned that this, too, was a lie

To mark a shroud of brutal pointless coffin, with a love song and a story telling,

With blades, like runes, to show us that this is always home.
That say, I too, remember.

I am owl-headed, a turnaround, a gift. And I know that Nessie left
Behind his casing on the loch-floor. Is he following some

Wisdom that remains? Beyond the self-absorbed humanizing
Of us all? Our manifest invisibility?
The fathers all died, as men are apt to do, from the wounds of other men

While those who stay are bewildered as cattle that have lost their voices to a careless abattoir.

Women in black dresses and feet no longer calloused from freedom,

Still write their letters of calling, to Mag Tuired or the Somme.

I reach into your sludge and pull out gold from deep
Within the pit of ancestral loam. Oaks incalculable once turned to war

Now bound in the hull of drowned ships.
And I am them, a thread of linen picked, kept quiet in the nests of ravens,

Landed—stranded for a while—within a bleaching bright, unfamiliar day

Until a piper summons bears to wake the salmon and drink the honey...

So that, now, and until drenched in distant children
No one—not anyone—can forget.

> *May your trails be crooked, winding, lonesome, dangerous,*
> *leading to the most amazing view.*
> *May your mountains rise into and above the clouds.*
>
> *—Edward Abbey*

...

TAKE THE DARKENED ROAD

Take the darkened road, love. But carry a light. Them mountains in the distance is you, forgotten. Them voices singin ancient lullabies, now, is you, too. On a wind that shrieks, threadbare, through weaving winding, rubble strewn alleys, through broken forests of dead hope. Now, laments of broken glass, discarded needles, a meth pipe and the bottom of a bottle at wine o'clock, rememberin when she promised, *nah, it won't never be me*, and she lied, because she couldn't keep hope up.

'Crack it', the mountains say, 'this code of us. This face was never pretty, and our inheritance to you is in the shadow of every judgment without grace. Use it, the discernment. Just don't spread it too thin. No popes or unchanging governments gonna help you. Got no light, ya see? Just the mad poets and singers of songs and tellers of stories with a little *deep* to em. We got you.

No tables set with silver, but these crusts are buttered. Necessary initiation, did I mention? Tippin yer hat to it, is to become a grownup. Bring a bit of who you truly are to the feast. Oh, and honest lore? Where's the next true tongue comin from, and is the water of the river you drink from as clean as it seems?'

Travel the darkened road, you will, that's just a certain thing. But carry a light, love, cause there's others along the way, be dark, and take too much, eh? Be careful to know what you know, and not guess.

Us mountains're tired of people

        gotta climb us to think emselves worthy.

        We'll say it again...

        ...

STORIES TO CRACK THE TARMAC

Understand: stories are lore made accessible. You hear them or you read them and then you ask the storyteller to teach you what they really mean. And, this can take many years, and, because of that, there is, currently in the world as we know it, a bit of a problem. Folks and wildlings, scholars even, have you stopped asking the questions? Challenging the purveyors of authority? Challenged the spooky shop with lots of products to sell, misappropriated, or cheap and sparkly but that cost a bundle of wisdom to purchase? That cost a whole lack of integrity that we're expected to accept as okay.

With only tired stories that even *they* know are not deep enough. Seems people are passing these tales along, of some deity or another, this remedy or that, as literal, and no one is reminding you that they are lying. Even while you scrunch your brow. How are they different to the missionaries that shove a *bible* down the throats of forest people, followed by soap and a beating?

Then grownups, the initiated ones, and the few elders left in the world (the ones not shoved into nursing homes because they no longer care to speak) know the stories are deep-time history. Are lore. That they are not clothed in predictable, acceptable and cool Jungian archetypes, because lots of us are from an altogether different ancestral lineage. Brer Rabbit does not fit the 'hero' role... and he's not Brer Rabbit after all.

So, take a break.

Question the rhetoric being chucked at you as truth. Challenge what the fuck are *underworlds* and *cauldrons* and *yule*, eh? Because how can they be real? And if they *are* real, what, then do they really mean?

Because... and here's the secret... things are more. And that *more* is honest language. Honest language'll hurt, have no doubt. But initiation is a potent thing, I promise.

Who are we, when those scales are peeled from our tired eyes?

...

CROWHEARTED

It seems like an illness. This weird pitter-patter music where a heart should beat. Rain overflowing the gutter in a steady, zen-garden-bamboo-night rain tonkle. I think I was maybe three, when crow first tore into me and took away the capacity to grow into other kids. Set up this nest. A thing that felt like awe. A scarring that I'm proud of.

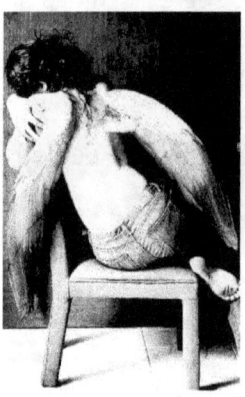

Later on, they paired up. In love for life. Year after year, breeding storytellings into the dreams of others, a bit like I was becoming. Having me live 'em first though. And that was hard. Fledgling, working out what wings are for, along the airwaves of the world. I must say predators took a lot out of me. Traps and poison culled... is culled the right word for taking importances away? Culled hundreds of things I had to say. Of *who* I am, who we thought we were. Yeah, you too, you know yourself to be like this, eh? Talking to you about you... What? You thought I'd leave you out of the story? Not ever gonna happen, friend.

I have a crow inside me instead of a heart. A blackness that is some kind of beauty. Some of you got the same thing. Some of you know what I'm saying. When this wildness savages the *uglies* that people try to plant in you, and who call 'em truth, a bit of us can die. The rest has to learn how to fight. To be a warrior for the wake. We peck 'em to death and refuse to eat the carcass, cause of the wrongness in it. The wrongness they tried to tell us that we are. I can circle all that in a mess of midnight-blue pinions, and scavenge behind them, into their secrets, where the good stuff hides and not what they have discarded.

Crows are corvids. Like ravens and jays and jackdaws. Like magpies and rooks. Making the world new every day. Shot. Maligned. Why?

We've heard it said our chatter is a fucken racket. But it's really a language that people don't know—don't recognize as something—because they only hear the voices of the red blood hearts, so easily broken, so casually betrayed. We're having a meaningful conversation when we sit on the barbed wire or the electricity lines, or on top of streetlights, calling to the families two miles away that here's the black plastic bag, rattling in the wind, all chokkas with food, calling sunset, and no predators in this part of the city.

It's a funny thing... Is it funny? That people think we caw cacophonously. When what's going on is really particularly important. Like where's the food? Who's dead? Who's in charge? What's a true name? Where's the bloke with the rifle? How the fuck did you open the bag with the velcro?

Crow instead of a heart. Hackle feather sloughing off, and making for ground zero, every season. Black thing as wild as the days people hide from. Too hot, too cold. Why can't we control this? Why am I not lucky? Why am I so poor? How can I get more likes? Why did a son abandon me?

Some big ol' Birch and Cedar and Spruce forest. That's where crow is from. The maker of the world. The waddler across the asphalt. The wickedness on the beach at Bettystown, County Meath, when shouldn't they be seagulls scavenging the tourist chips, and not us big ol' blackbirds?

The one thing I'm pretty sure about is this, if you're crowhearted as well, nothing is going to seem ordinary. Bits are interesting. Stuff people chuck away make good nest material. Things look different. Talk is not the same.

When crow ate that bit of me, and set up home, I didn't know anything was wrong. It was like this for everybody. Then I thought I was a mad kid. I didn't know what ribbons of flight felt like, then. Not for years. Thought I'd died. I could have. I just never put it down to an experience I ever recognized from anybody else. When I was big enough, I wrote poetry. Things of the dead. Of god. Of fearing and wanting to know what it really means to not be. Why people kill each other. Even if they don't think they do. Cruelty like that. Crows feed on stuff like that.

Crow instead of a heart. Had to figure out how to sing with that voice. Something like laryngitis. Like there were thorns in what I said when all of it was love. Talking crow comes out strange to lots of people, most of the time. And funny. Funnyfunny and dangerous together. Like chili-chocolate is, like desire for trinkets and bright, shiny-seeming friendships that turn bitter as easy as pissing.

Some kind of mystery tore a hole in normal that night, when I was just a chicken. While I was sleeping. When I was a kid, in that dream, and… was shown a deep valley, to soar through once I worked out what wings were for. Pond water to drink from. Gutter water. Leftover water from storm water type water. Breeding ground am I, for generations yet to be born. And there. That's the bottomlessness of being corvidhearted, isn't it?

Poetry from some wizened, scary, dark, un-chainsaw'd forest elder lore. Does it take a long time to get a head around all this? If I'm still working at that, I bet you are too.

But. What I know? What I realize? I'm awfullyawfully glad. About crow, that is. I have no idea what *normal* must beat like. A bloody-great big, raggedy, black-feathered crow of a bird, where a heart once was... isn't such a bad way to grow up after all.

...

THE NAME OF THE WORLD IS ALIVE

Objectification of the natural world reinforces the notion that our species is somehow more deserving of the gifts of the world than the other 8.7 million species with whom we share the planet. Using "it" absolves us of moral responsibility and opens the door to exploitation. When Sugar Maple is an "it" we give ourselves permission to pick up the saw. "It" means it doesn't matter.

—Robin Wall Kimmerer

AUTHENTICITY

The tradition and ritual of naming a human person is to bestow identity and authenticity.

Amongst indigenous cultures the practice of naming is not only to attach a meaningful identity to the newly alive individual but also to confer a place upon them: of wetlands, seasonal shapeshiftings, thin-iced fjords and desert vastnesses realized only by a night filled with star myth. Maps of ancient territory, they are numbered amongst ancestors from whom we have all unfurled or been spawned.

Often naming relates to an elder's family and inherited profession: smith, archer, bell, faulkner, falconer, weaver, potter, hunter, dyer and cooper, reiver. Prior—even adjacent—to this is the association of the born individual's clan and lineage. Their homeland and the spirit of that home: coombe, brook, cairn, forest, gold. Rain. Snow. Summer.

Naming is, or was, a profound and welcoming endowment and embrace. A nest from which to train wings. A burrow within which to sharpen claws. The process opening a page into some spoken, danced or sung unwritten book of wisdom's lore, of future knowledge; of heritage.

Naming should not be bestowed lightly. Lazily. Expediently. It is never the right of strangers to impose upon a person for a whim, or a vanity. No one is a package to be owned.

Bitu [1], Life, has endowed us, as a hominid species, with the odd, quizzical habit of naming everything. Those of us termed *westerners* utilise 80% nouns, often gendered, to objectify and push away from us—or to seemingly force outside of us—our relatives of fur and fin and feather, of stone and weather and sídhe, and therefore deny relationships with everyone of other genii, spirits of place, as well as ourselves, including our mothers and grandfathers... and even winter.

CARELESS AGE

But we have become careless. Populist. The journey from the deepest roots of an ancestral tree does not name me niCunobelin; does not name me Loðbrok Sigurddottir's daughter or the now-born ancestral child of the Gothic *barbarian* Alaric 1st, or of Audreé de Romenel (de Jarpenville), Sergeant of the Hawk in 1207, Paris. But there I am... yes, here I am.

Offspring are named something popular, or kitsch, the last names of many of us in the so-called western civilization—*freeonama* [2]— broken down into meaninglessness, with no threads to weave us into deeptime's mother-blanket. Clan, tuath, the skill of the Reindeer herder, the carvers and Raisers of stone menhirs (navigational markers, meant to never end up as gravel on a highway), the knowledge of whiteness or verdancy of landscape and what to plant or hunt or forage and when, what fogs will kill, what fungi are edible.

The *pens* of coastlines, embracing Cornwall, that are safe to anchor at, are nowadays rendered of little significance, careless frippery like

a barcode tattooed on a soft inner arm... or is that a number I see? Oh, okay, an identifying mark worthy only of a mere glance, read by some bureaucrat and meant to bestow legitimacy and *authenticity*; a status of *owned-by*, on a newly born human being. Rendering those we thought to love open to bullying and jeers.

> *Just as nature's names are vanishing from the language of children, nature itself is vanishing. Forgetting is an easy way to lose things – as each generation becomes more at ease with less nature, we forget what it is that we've lost.*
>
> —Robert Macfarlane.

Dr Robert Macfarlane, scholar, rewild reminder and author of passivity-defying works of responsibility, of whom I am an ardent groupie, is referring to the removal of many words, around 2017, from the *Oxford Junior Dictionary*, that include Acorn, Adder, Ash, Beech, Bluebell, Buttercup, Dandelion, Heron, Otter and Willow. There are many more. And...

> *The Lost Words grew out of research for his book Landmarks (2015), which examined the work of a dozen British and American writers of place, and gathered and organized over 2,000 terms for nature, landscape, creatures and weather from more than 30 languages, dialects and sub-dialects of Britain and Ireland.*
>
> —University of Cambridge [3]

GENIUS LOCI

A name becomes a glue that can embellish, or destroy, one's sense of uniqueness. Like St Kilda.

Most people in australia think it's the name of a football club or a

beachside suburb of melbourne. The full name *st kilda* first appeared on a dutch 1666 nautical map that might be derived from the norse words *sunt kelda: sweet well water*. The island, deep within the wild north sea of the outer Hebrides, known as *Hirta*, bearing no equality to anything sainted. There was never a *st kilda*.

An icelandic saga describes an early 13th-century voyage to ireland that mentions a visit to the islands of *hirtir* (norse for *stag*) so that the name may be derived from the shape of the island which is said to resemble our species cousin [4]. Also: Gaelic *í árd* (high island).

Is any of this important?

I don't remember where I read about the Albanach warriors, at the battle of Culloden, chanting the names of their matrilineal ancestors as a taunt to the mindlessness of cultural plunder that sat, grinning with greed and saddled safely at the rear of their 3,000 terrified English soldiers, but sometimes I think I'm too old to recall most of what I once learned. I think I read about it in Loren Cruden's book *Walking the Maze*. Whether that is so or not, it stirs the blood to think so. Just like bagpipes being played within dense fog, somewhere close enough to haunt. Just like the thunder of a hundred bódhrans, three minutes past midnight on the eve of Samhain. Like the scratching, insistent sound of some small, stealthy critter-claws; the footfall of a someone-animal who should not be walking across your pillow in the dark of your bedroom, that rouses you from sleep in an instant of terror and wakefulness.

Living elders, of indigenous people, would no more simply introduce themselves by their English-endowed names of *jackie*, or *king billy* than they would willingly take their own lives in the holding cell of a northern territory prison. If they do it is because they can see no way to continue to belong. No ancestor at their backs to remind them of honour and *ghebh–* (a proto-Indo-European root word meaning to give or receive, thought also to represent *to hold*). Fitting, is the introduction of tribe, legend, tuath and living mountain, the naming of ancestors of renown and even affiliations with intermarital families before adding, *Oh, and I'm called Alice Muggle, and I'm in I.T.*

NAMING IS TREACHEROUS

When, and if, a person changes their name from what has been written on any government-sanctioned document, like a birth certificate or a passport, they always do so for a specific reason. A self-claiming. A denial of those, with whom they share DNA, because of differences of opinion, ideology or self-determinism. Because an unsurpassable chasm has cracked the landscape open. Bereft of compassion. Lost love. A trans man, who was named Michelle at birth, sure of self and proud of their identity, denied by those with a creed to which they cling and whose ears defile vitality with a bigotry. Like the inside of a coffin, long after the worms have done their work of nourishing the future, with the body of your beige and withered grandmother supposedly packaged for resurrection when *jesus* remembers the covenant. What's left. What's husk. The ghost. The manitou. A *disnified* princess who was, in truth, an Altai shaman buried in the permafrost of an Arctic mountain, beneath four horses, before someone at Wikipedia became offended at her *ness*. An intentional internet *oopsie*.

Ignoring the ferocity voiced by the person who does not acknowledge a name such as *michael* (printed on the christian residential school admission form[5]), whose Anishinaabe mother named them *Waawaate*, for the Northern Lights that wove so bright within the midwinter night of this newborn human being's birth.

Any number of righteous and honest reasons ignored through the pretense of privilege.

WIZARDS OF AUTHENTICITY

But what is lost? Or is this story one of hiddenness? And is that Which has been buried under the terrible weight of a religious and Anglican cosmology, that excludes all who do not fit the orthodox, conventional or conservative zeitgeist, able to be exhumed?

Arborists of hominid pedigrees. Genealogists. Twenty-first century druids. Wizards of authenticity. Topographers of identity-mapping. Finders of the wanderer dying for water.

I am given identity by this person in this house. He has traced me[6]. Mapped an ancestral course of names and migrations and decimations, through seas that are rocky and dark with unseen dangers. And I have not foundered. Navigated with all of me. Ancestors extant by the simple fact of being here. A lifetime of namelessness liberated. Is it done? Are we there yet? No.

But the gate has been crashed, the dust blown off the dismembered heads still trapped within the museum archives. The loading has begun, and the re-gardening of Babel agreed to, albeit with a bitter hesitation.

I have a false identity to kill with honesty and another to claim for the same reason. I've known this prison of archaic labelling and be fucked if I'll retain it. With a second-last breath I'll deny it and with the last... I WILL rename it.

What is the wellspring of your name? Do you know it? Was it stolen? Are you still proud or is it a withered, gummy throw-away bit of nothing?

> *Yes, I received your letter yesterday, about the time the doorknob broke When you asked me how I was doing, was that some kind of joke All these people that you mention, yes,*

> *I know them, they're quite lame I had to rearrange their faces and give them all another name Right now, I can't read too good, don't send me no more letters no Not unless you mail them from Desolation Row.*
>
> —Bob Dylan, *Desolation Row*, 1965.

How many chances do we get?

Who are you?

If it does not matter then neither do you. When the story is spoken and completed for now, and the crowd has left for the dawn, it might be nothing. The sun—this solar star amongst the incalculable—goes nova, someday, after all.

...

[1] The Proto-Celtic term *bitu* "world" connotes the place of "life" (Proto-Celtic *biwotūt*). Source
[2] Old English: free name/family name, first recognized in the 14th century, although realized within Norman culture from the 12th century. Source https://www.etymonline.com/word/surname
[3] https://www.cam.ac.uk/thelostwords
[4] Island on the Edge of the World, Charles Maclean, 1977, p 33
[5] https://www.etymonline.com/word/michael
[6] Genealogy: www.thesignsofthetimes.com.au
Source: https://www.yesmagazine.org/issue/together-earth/2015/03/30/alternative-grammar-a-new-language-of-kinship/

SINGING CONCRETE FROM SLEEP

Staring into this cup a coffee I get visions of your disquiet and understand your frustration. Your house is not earth rammed and thatched by your father and uncles. Your shoes are not hooves and your hair no longer maiden-fern, spilling from the crevice beside the water.

You are dumbstruck by words that are not howls and snarls. Your skin is rubbing your bones because the woodland is beyond you. You cannot answer the *bansídhe* call because you have appointments with someone else in a zoo. Instead, you shriek in the peep of silent hawk-*ness* and you scratch at the iron door with painted talons.

We get ya. Keep faith, Puppies. A thousand years from now... promises never broken... you'll know.

...

DID SOME FOOL SAY FOLLOW YOUR DREAMS?

You wake up and wonder who you are. Where you are. You've been sitting at a bus stop on a busy city street when the UFOs come. Hundreds of them. Descending at great speed. You momentarily think, cool... Before you realize they are going to destroy everything, so you run.

Over field, hill and valley, fighting to breathe, thinking *where are the children? Please. Please. Let them have found a place to hide!*

    LOST AND ALONE

You are shaken awake. By a stranger in a white uniform who tells you to come and get your dinner. And you look in the mirror, heart still pounding with that dread you just experienced, that you will never, never see your family again. Your hair is black. Long. But your face is lined with the roadmap of an eighty year old woman. Or older. And you wonder, fleetingly, if you still dye your hair. But you can't remember.

You go to tea, and you recall, with even greater dread than the dream, that you are in an old people's home. A one-way door to the grave. And how, dear mother-mercy, did this happen?

Only *then* do you wake up.

Maybe...

I think, really, what is meant by *follow your dreams* is...

1. work your hoodoo like crazy to make something happen.
2. don't trust the fool who says *follow your dreams.*
3. learn everything and miss nothing.
4. please, Wildling, be strong enough to retain faith in yourself.

...

HUSH LI'L BABY

Child of this here woman, a woman now y'self, with them big firm milky breasts and them old blue jeans, do your mama a kindness and sit with me here on the stoop while you suckle that baby. Hold em gentle, but hold em tight, just the same. While I tell you a story you best not forget.

Today I drove past an empty lot. Home gone. Garden. Everything. Razed to the ground.

Surrounded by stormproof wire fencing. Not a week ago a big old house was there. Big brick place with a chimney and a veranda, rose bushes brought all the way from Europe, and lavender, and plum and apple trees just about to blossom. All gone now.

Woulda been built before that war, that massacred all those sons of mine. *Righteous war*, some liar called it. Sons gunned down on a forsaken beachhead, cigarette still stuck behind an ear for later. Children herded onto cattle trains. Jews and Roma. Homosexuals (they called you that back then) and academics, people just thinking *why?* out loud. Burned in ovens. Ashes and nameless suitcases in a pile, abandoned. All those others buried under rubble in London and in Dresden. Maralinga.

What, you say? Get to the point, Mama?

Your other nipple's leakin, child. Rub that goodness into baby's skin. That's the way. Point is, it could be you. From the day you and loverboy plan it, from a hope in your eyes to when the gate gets screwed to the fence post. Where your kids get born, one after the other, you and him sweatin neath the covers, them brats irrelevant to the love makin.

Then they've all gone, and you're set to wanderin from room to room, insane with confusion, cause it is all still so fresh and yesterday, mumblin softly, *Come back, you come see Mama some time. Please?* And they will for a while. When they remember.

Now your house is gone. Everything. You too. And I drive past on the way to live this life as wildly and as witchingly, and as irreverently as I can, child of mine. So don't you suss me for it! Because that's what I got. It's what you got. It's what your baby's got. And that's all we got. In the so-called Once Upon a Time...

Now I'm gonna put the kettle on and make us both a brew. And you're gonna snuggle yer baby down warm in the cradle. Then you gonna join me in the kitchen, even though there's nothin left to talk about, for years and years.

And then once. Always, it's just once. You're gonna hug me, and hold me, as gentle and as hard as you can.

...

UPPITY WHITE WOMAN

OR IS SHE, PERHAPS, SNOW?

Mother tried to drown me when I was born. Our culture does not allow an albinist child to live. Bad luck. Pointless hunting would be the fault of allowing me to live. I'd dry up the milk of cattle. I'd be responsible for shrivelling the penises of men, and be the reason babies are spat from a womb not a month into pregnancy. I would remind them of days hoped gone forever. Stone and antler cave days. I reminded them of who we truly were before the world seemed to become tame. I arrived, unfortunately for her, at the time of the deep, dark, frozen cold.

But Father, crow-black hair and amber-eyed, a mouth full of laughter, strong-armed and deep-voiced—stopped her, and spirited me away. He took me to Penwith, a *miniwikin* not long birthed of a dead person, her big, full breasts futilely overflowing and causing her grief. He carried me through fear-high drifts of snow, keeping me alive bundled in goose feather pillows and fox skins, and he dropped me down into the midwife's lap, even without her say-so. Men. Go figure what they see in some of us? He told me later that her eyes went wide with both fear, and that other thing that happens to some at the sight, smell, and touch of a newborn, though mewling, violet-eyed kitten of a kid that I was. She told me, in later years, that her milk dripped right off, making cold the front of her smock, right down to the tool belt.

There I was. Like a limpet sucking sustenance from a tide-bound rock pool.

Mother raged at Father when he got back to the dun. *Dimwit! Call yourself a king? For goodness sake, you're supposed to be a man! It'll be the laughingstock! Don't you dare ever say it came out of me, I'll have your balls on this breakfast toast quicker'n you can squeal, you muthafuckin, wetnosed, nostalgic wimp of a monarch.* And she'd not humped him for weeks.

Well, I just kept on being a white-as-winter two-legged, left to myself most of the time, or else hanging out with the dogs. I got no evil eye from the villagers: not goodwife nor hunter, blacksmith or tanner. Nor any of the animals neither. Especially not Spud. As pale as me, he is, but nobody ever gives him a hard time for the color he was born to. He's big as a pony and destined to head the sled team when he's fully trained in the traces. Life's been me and him from as far back as I can remember.

Mother... what's her name again? You know those words that are so cruel on the tongue you forget them on purpose somehow? Like widow-makers. You know what they are? Sometimes hunters pitch a tent for the night, sheltering till brother blizzard passes, then crack, in their sleep, that massive lower branch snaps under the weight of too much ice, killing every one inside.

A bit too smart for your own good, is what Penwith says, time and again, when I say stuff like that about the woman who bore me, who I occasionally see at a distance—at the market or down by the pier, at the ships, bringing treasure from the East. Penwith suggests I keep thoughts like that to myself, but who am I supposed to tell anyway? Other kids? *The* other kids? I'm as white as the *fullwinter* snow and not even a freckle to break up the ghost of me. No. Other children learned early not to even peek towards me. Playing is what sled dogs are for. Spud and the others.

Mother glances from a distance. I know who you are, Mother. By your crown. Narrow heavy metal line around hair the color of a dangerous autumn forest, eyes hooded, as though you'd rather not see me. I'm supposed to be dead; I realize that. A thin line to your lips suggests what? Hatred? Your gaggle of honey-skinned other children, their hair as black as Father's, dressed in finely-woven, woad-dyed wool, silk-lined ermine, and bear fur for their shoulders, walking behind you with the grace that the privileged are taught at your knee. At your command. None of them know about me, do they?

Father keeps the *miniwikin* in ample stock. For payment, I guess. Not that Penwith cares. I was her pride right from the getgo, and only her own mother and Robert the Axe—the man who loves her and shares her bed—knows. And even though Robert is *the* best woodsman for mile after vast mile, keeping the houses in the dun, and outer walls of the longhouse loaded high with deep-seasoned redwood and spruce logs, peeled and quartered perfectly, he could never be paid the kind of meat that Father could provide, so he cedes me being raised by Midwife Penwith with humble grace.

That was that, and all fine, for ten or more years. I ran with Spud and the other dogs, learned the way of the sled like a navvie, if not like a musher. I could chew rawhide to soft leather with the best of 'em. And I gained an education in *miniwikin*, to the point I can identify and name every healing wort, and gathering-green, in all the valleys and on all the mountainsides, for miles and miles. I know everything from how to lance the pus from a wound, to what it takes to pull a calf from her mother, legs first.

And then I hit about twelve, I guess. I get underarm hair and even more at groin. Small round mounds where nipples, until now, have been of little consequence. I keep this a secret, of course, as I figure it to be trouble, there not being *anything* I haven't seen that people with such get up to, me traveling with Penwith and the sled dogs, to near a cabin for a birth or a death. Me watching from the tree line. Taboo. Getting an education from a distance. I understand rutting—sex, that people tend to call mating—same for a person as for a dog and a horse, or caribou and reindeer in season. Same as foxes and wolves.

People, and me too if I'm honest, are so used to me hiding out and

being this kid who disappears into the color of winter, that I'm just part of the landscape, because there is no hunting more pointless than sometimes happens anyway, there is no drying up the milk of cattle and, from what Penwith jokes about, no shrivelling of the penises of men or babies spat out of women's wombs only a month or two from when they get planted.

But then I have hair that has taken on the light of butter, and that, within a year, turns amber, a little lighter than Mother's, and I have to think of what to do next. Now, at night, I am able to be seen when I hunt with Spud. And the blood has begun. Ho. What a curse is womanhood, eh?

Worried out of her brain about all this, Penwith sends for the six other *miniwikins* of the region, and she banishes Robbie to the forest when they come, saying *go cut a brother down or something for a week, love. Shape something beautiful with your axe and knives, okay?* because he is trained in forest lore, not woman magic, and therefore, for now, this is not about him The *miniwikins* come together one dark December night, well after midwinter and, after they've had copious cups of mushroom tea, I'm called inside from where I'm grooming the puppies in the byre. I sit on a stool in the firelight from the hearth, surrounded by these women, from smooth-skinned to leather-barked, all hung about with copper and bone talismans. All belted with stoppered, sap-collecting jars and, despite the warmth of the cottage, are swathed from head to foot in fur and woven linen, their skin covered voluminously in scars of sooty ink.

Penwith is the eldest, though not as skin-wrinkled as the others close to her age, because she's big and round from the cuts of kill Father delivers. The best fat, the liver, the intestines. Whatever he can snaffle from the dispersion.

How much miniwikin she got? was the main question asked over the

tobacco smoke from their pipes. *Fire and dog*, proclaims Penwith. *Best dog magic EVER*. That gets nods and pouts, lips scrunching like bums. It means there is a use for me. A really good thing under the circumstances, and it is all round agreed that if I ever get to looking any more like Mother she's going to get pissed and deadly. Like winter not wanting to give way to spring.

So, what's a *miniwikin* to do?

They stay for six more nights, and every night I am made to sit with head in hands and listen to the *how* of tracking a way to each demesne where they abide, that each of them describes. Every landscape, every river. This twisted tree, that standing stone between two hills, the cove between two headlands that looks like horns holding the moon, the lake with stones that lead to the island in the middle—but only in autumn and before the leaves fell. The road made by mules, to-ing and fro-ing from the salt mines, bowed low enough to become tarmac. Lore. Maps. I learn those places by shutting up and just listening.

Then, one night not long after, Father comes, a bundle in his arms: a cloak of tanned mammoth so soft it's like a dream remnant, despite its size. Sharp knives and scissors, needles of whalebone, the makings necessary to craft shafts, the bow already cured from last year's ash. A cooking pot. A warning. A nod to Penwith. A whispered message to Robbie. Then a look. He gives me a look. Something that, should I become snaggle-toothed, I will always remember. Is that love?

It has come to this. The hounds are hugged one-by-one, except for Spud, untethered and walking with me, the only companion for the long haul. Midwife Penwith smelling deep into my lungs, her body enfolding me like I was fingers in her mittens, in that night of the midnight sun, just before the season turns towards the light again. Me and Rob, side by side, huffing white air into white air.

Robbie picks up a trail of the spoor of a parcel of deer. A day and a night hunting the straggler. I shoot. He guts and skins. We share the eating of the heart. He stows the liver and the lungs in his satchel.

You, he explains.

For her? I respond, knowing the answer is yes.

...

I love you, Snow, is all he says as I run towards the escarpment, aware that I will never see him, or Penwith, or Father, ever again. And deep, deep in the guts of me, feeling an ache that will last forever.

...

Now I live in a small house on the shore of Loch Sgadabhagh, on the island of North Uist, amidst the Innse Gall—*the islands of the strangers*—amidst the dottings of the Outer Hebrides of the coast of what is rudely called Scotland. Mothers, fathers and I have been here since long before the Vikings came, surviving it all. Enough to set the story straight, told elder to child, *miniwickin* to *miniwickin* until nobody knows the word anymore. Except us.

I am generations down the boon-line from being *Snow White*, or *Snow* of any color for that matter, but I'm still her. Although I have a very freckled face, I am the same woman. And no matter what gets thrown at her she, too, survives. Of course: no prince, no dwarves, no glass coffin, no ebony, because what peasant knows about these things, way off on the continent, and a thousand years beyond the truth of it all? Winter thought of as a wicked, jealous queen, a bane to other women. A bad name.

brothers and sisters are still in the world somewhere. And we have never met. We probably have such different stories and such different histories. If I could sit with them—kindred—we could watch each other's faces as we tell the way of legend… well, I can only dream.

The apple? The food that the shape-shifting wild weather, written of as a *step*-mother, really is? The poison words, that were just another way of killing me when Robbie's deceit was uncovered? Each successive trick failing until the wicked last—that I am the pretty possession of some wealthy man…?

That apple, I think, is still lodged in the throat of the *miniwickin*, cut by the pen of the gatherers of what are, spuriously, called *fairy stories* for children. By such pompous, grim, Grimm men, and published into popularity, for the reading by girl-children, and so to fool them into believing that someone will rescue them… from what exactly? And that when the desolation of happy-ever-after becomes known for the propaganda it is?

But *money talks* and, well, you know the rest of it. Isn't that how the saying goes? There's a price to be paid for hiding. For fearing winter.

…

NEVER A GOD

Just so we're clear, in case the word pops up anywhere in the following stories, *god* is not a person.

A god does not have a true name, and *god* is not a *god*, as we have been indoctrinated to think of a *god*. They have no gender, and they are never an *it*. They're an *us*... and we are not just human-bodied people.

Just so you know, if I use the word *god*, I don't mean a deity. Because I have no religion. I do not worship. We are belonging. In the way of present-continuous. *God* is the whole, being the sum of parts, but not greater than them. *God* is the land you are and have been since before you were recognizably human, and that of your ancestors of every species, of every flora, of every river, each wave upon the sand of an atoll. Each susurration that laps the shingles of a Cornish beach. The macaw within the Brazilian canopy. The blue fungus that teaches the dreamer sight. What you know of that. That the fungus knows you. The names of plants and the plants that are unknown and unnamed. That you are them, long after the body you inhabit ceases to be the *you* people think you are now. Or even that *you* think you are.

God is love and wildfires and volcanic eruptions. But there can be many. I think Neil Gaimon's *American Gods* comes close. The premise of that story is that migrating people bring the spirits of the old lands with them, and very often, over generations, those people forget. These *gods* are then up to whatever tricks they choose, to remain significant. Even simply among themselves.

A *god* can be a certain rock, along the *Birdsville* track in Australia, when there was no *Birdsville* track. That rock is a wayshower. Their name is sung and danced and painted by indigenous people who know that to pass by, and head north at a certain time of year, will lead them (and with the guidance of many other such *gods*) to the trading bay with the people who travel the sea routes (also *gods*) from elsewhere for that trade.

Now we have established what I intend, should I use the *god* word anywhere in this (or any other book). When a tall, dark-skinned man named Hunter, introduces himself as a forest *god*, he doesn't necessarily say which Forest. And he only appears to be a *he*. He is everything in the forest and, as such, could be any forest. At any time. Could also be the forest long since devastated for logging. Forgotten except as myth.

As you work your way through this lore, this gathering of teachings, this story-telling—or murder—of ravens, please spare a thought for the effect any of us have on a *god*, or the many *gods*, if we grade a road and remove that stone on the *Birdsville*, bulldoze a Forest (a *god*) and cover the Earth (a *god*) with concrete, build a dam where a free River (a *god*) once ran, construct a city, desecrate the bones of ancestral dead, of any species, terrorize the penned herds (*gods*) that are descended from what once were seasonally migrating Aurochs. Spare a thought pertaining to our ignorance at treading roughshod over what has lived for a million years. That makes us, also *gods*, yes? What kind of *gods* are we? What kind of *god* communes with me?

Just for a moment, let us consider this because, in the time of the second era of mass extinctions, those being driven extinct are also *gods*. And their silence is deafening.

When I meet a wild *god*, it is as likely to be the bricks in the wall that were once the clays along the Riverbed. True magic is in listening and acknowledgment. Of everyone, unconscionably called a "thing". To be the grains of Sand that are the gods of future Atolls, holding stories within their warmth for when the next Ice Age sets us free to remember.

BONE MAGIC

Life has dragged you along a raggedy track belonging to the wolf. A long-neglected landscape, gathering the fur and feathers and bones of dry, dusty and archived myth, glamoring it anew in garments of mist and Hedge-rose, the silver fleck of black-muscled Salmon in the pool beneath the gnarled and ancient Hazel. The roan hide of a many-tined Stag, trumpeting from the far glen that he is back from the brink.

I'm alive to recognize your isolation and, once seen, to then conjure the word-druidry that I know can show you home. To remind you to be *god*. I've been death's companion since I was born, you know, but she waited like a lady. "Here," she says softly, when I am old enough for it, "have a pen, little girl. Let's see what you can do if I agree to you staying a while."

Wasn't any *god* then. Wasn't any *god* for years. Wasn't any *god* till I knew what a *god* isn't. Till I recognized a *god* in the way the weather tells the truth. Till I realized it could be anything, any one of you, just as long as I keep eyes wide open and ears *undeaf* until I hear you.

And I've got work cut out for me to remind you of the fact that you ARE *gods*. What a responsibility is *that* for you? That all of you make the picture bigger. Just like mountains. Just like sand. Just like air and yesterday.

I'll live doing this; die still doing this.

...

YOU CAN HEAR THE FREEDOM

We walk straight. Offensive, yes? You think you've done enough to bend our backs and shut us up?

We walk tall.

Don't kid yourself for a minute there's no inside and outside cause there is.

Who do you know on the outside?

Us? You think you know us?

We walk tall.

And you see us, but nothing registers. Only calculation. Only a stranger. Difference is suspicion, taught in kiddy school. Being outside is a force of nature and a shudder of *notness*. Your apartment, your suburban block, is today's cave, some remembered acknowledgment, maybe? A coffin, maybe. A prison with no blackness, therefore TV counts as placation. But shh! No deliverance of ochre and bone-lore here folks.

What you see, when you look at us, is what you been taught. Shabby, says someone. Dangerous, says a neighbor, leaning on the shovel from where he dug himself that pit, after signing a paper, held, hand out, sinister smile and greedy, wanton byte of digi-currency hiding profit, by someone else who had as much right to land as he was told he could have. A right to torture in the name of L'Oréal. To dredge the ocean floor, for the slurry in them vats, to feed the children of a remembered sea, for your prawn curry. Never thinking should I ask more questions? Do I get away with it? This rule of might? You shut your mouth and take this unanswer. Just in case there is an answer.

There is an answer.

INSIDE OUT

Outside. What is outside, in difference to inside? Is inside safe?

As safe as it'll ever be. Like a zoo. Like the 44th floor of a building, seconds before a 7.2 echo of human-style morbidity, renders the unwritten agreement with a dead deity and a mortgage manager, pointless, in the glow of the Richter scale.

You're on the inside. That makes you rich, yes? And free to get a good haircut. To put your kids in school where they can never learn, but will make a living selling cars, or as slab designers for cheaper tower block construction. Or researchers who will one day, one day maybe, cure cancer. Without ever asking what, inside this fucking bubble, causes cancer in the first place. You know about Mỹ Lai, Fukushima, Bobby Sands, Adam Goodes, Emily Wilding Davison. You won't make that mistake again. Learned, is learned.

What do you see? How did you, on the inside, see us, on the outside, as odd? What side of the broken-bottle-covered-dark-brick-wall protects you? From an eventual broken slab of Stone, or a plaque set in a wall somewhere, with a name on it, that used to mean you?

We walk straight, and that pisses one woman off. She's behind the plexiglass at the bank. Her look says, *You shouldn't be here*. And when I take the ribbon off the bundle of fifty-dollar bills, and slide the money across the counter, not taking these eyes from hers, she drops her gaze first, like a pretend-sleepy owl. Fucken ruse. Looks down and away from me, as if a predator has her already, bloody, in a metal-toothed trap, but to make a noise will only call the hunter. Is this a pretence of submission? Yes. No. Hatred likes to hide itself, a defence of similarities. It's a species-thing, I think.

Rattled. I watch her face as she smiles at the cash, like she wishes it could smile back. To justify herself. To stop from asking why I am what she is not, a denuding shame I will one day rectify. Or someone like me.

Despite her upbringing. Because of it.

Her eyes remain cemently downcast. She only lifts em to check the computer screen. She lets the flat pads of her fingers press each square on the keyboard, filling in necessary boxes. Black, taloned fingernails, that she paid shitloads to have glued to the real ones, that flaunt some kind of fashion warning. Fingers that can't—won't—skin a dead Rabbit, or pick grass seeds from between soft-hounded toes, or shoot a Kangaroo that's been careless, crossing a road that has recently sliced right through an ancient track that leads to the River; a track that's been journeyed for a hundred thousand years. Kangaroo, who's left crippled, her unborn child dying on the teat, inside her warmth-going-cold, insulted, uneaten flesh-and-blood body, silencing the question WHY into the dusk that knows, that always has and always will.

Woman-fingers that cannot light a fire to cook a meal to feed the kids, teaching them nothing of *imramma*. Of elder lore. Of fishing and dancing under moonlight. Too late, you'll wish it was yesterday, but it's already too late... The men have it. Are they the enemy? No. They learned like everyone else on her side of that one-sided prison wall.

Abandoned, confused, wandering the dream she lives in—gimme opium, laudanum, valium, anything but this—of once upon a time, when they've all gone. Living on a pension and white bread because she neglected to see the wonder of the loon and the lion, and the deathcap and the deep, uncrossable current on the outside. Freezing when the power is switched off. Desiccating in her stiff-sheeted, defecated, rubber-lined hospital bed, because that's it, folks. This's the payoff.

She doesn't like me.

How can I know that? It's the way, when she lifts her chin and sort of tilts her pretty head. Crucifix in gold (with a wee ruby), once, perhaps, received as a wedding gift, now shifting on her décolletage like it's alive with endless loss. The overhead light catching the retina of each thought. A microscope. One corner of her lips a megaphone to the deaf, screeching, *I don't like you. You shouldn't have money like this. You shouldn't look like that. Are you a... Um... a...* I turn a back to her as I walk out. I walk as straight as the rest of us. As tall, no matter the height I stand. On this outside to an otherwise inside species.

As I write this I ask, over and over, am I condescending? Fuck it, they got to me once too.

THE FREEDOM OF SPEARS, WOLVES AND EAGLES

What did Dylan sing? *When y'aint got nothin, you got nothin to lose.* Where'd he get the idea of stuff? What's nothin? Who thinks that way? The lady in the bank thinks that way. So does their boss. So, also, does theirs. And theirs. And theirs.

Nothin, he wrote, minding well the intentionally-distained g, an arrogant middle finger to monarch, and nation, I mean Australia. I mean America and Ireland. I mean the Torres Straight Islands and

Pipalyatjara. England, France, Germany, Palestine. Auschwitz, Wounded Knee, Slaughterhouse Creek, Stonewall. Who defines significance? Wherever a Chernobyl gives us hope before it remembers who heavy water is. Where heavy water belongs. No. Nothin is *terra nullius*. Some kind of favourite thing. Distribution: guns and smallpox, rape and uniforms. To the people who are not there, just passing, turning whiter with each violation. Every denial. Fuck me, speak English or iron my shirts. Your mother's Mother. Bring them inside. Isn't that it?

Who makes up this history? This righteousness? Who condones the killing of a river? Who consigns a forest to death, along with everyone who has ever lived with her since before Gondwana? Sanctifies the stealing of children? Indoctrination without their consent, because they got to please someone; to be acceptable to inside life. To serve.

GLUED TO BROKEN GLASS

It's not with any sense of pride that I scaled the fence and almost bled to death for who I'd mimicked. I just took it off... the garment of purpose I was told to wear. That lie. I reach across a chasm. Not white. Only nightshade and datura are white. This Blood and Flesh buried in another ancient land that others think forgets about me. When forever is never forgotten by its ownsomeness.

I'm not home, that's the reality, because the decimated ghostsland of forests and bears, that I am also, is so distressingly far away from here; lifetimes away from this red and black and thirsty land that takes nothing. That demands strength that is not ours to ripen into. That has everything taken. Me, that earth beneath the pole star, with the standing Stones and calligraphic ogham, where Badgers and Robins once dwelt in abandon, hasn't sunk yet, but it's only a matter of when. Has been stripped and raped and walked over with heavy boots and open sewers. With the simple fact of ermine, bibles and deportation. Dead woodland. Killed ancestors. Permission never given for either.

I am there because I'm here. We're there because we, also, are not yet sunk.

And mother, brother, grandmother wise-woman Shark, cruise the oceans between us landscapes, us creatures. Not fenced and farmed like the salmon who will never know muscle. I'm here because there's no way I want to be in, just to face it all. I'm here (a Milk Thistle beneath the asphalt, green as visible as that Nightshade before the springtime, only seen by critters of the darkness), to bend the knee to those whose eyes dream the long journey, despite massacres and white sugar, despite grog and meth.

With self, shining bright in the sky above ice and snowmelt, lonely pale creature, now, in the slippery, muddy walking tracks that I yearn for, but with Mist and Heather as mother and brother and milk and meat.

But, by all the forces of thunder and shine, walkin tall. Not a bowed back anywhere.

On the inside it's easy to hate. Aluminium rights, copper rights, sludge and mercury-poisoning rights. Rights taken, not given. *We built this fucking country from NOTHING. We have a right to the western suburbs dream, and fake nails that dig no dirt and pull no brumby from the burning. No racehorse from the abattoir. We don't need your fucking birthing tree. We got hospitals for that baby-borning-business, ya savage, Illiterate bastards that speak that language I don't understand, for which reason it must be ignorance. Therefore, it must cease, with whatever straight-backedness you think to offend me with. Now, get out of the way of the bulldozers or we'll imprison your arse. Where you can hang yourself with a shoestring. Or a plain old suffocation.*

Deadlock. Not bowing? *Someone's gonna die today*. Or so it is thought, if not said.

Land-and-body-death is a stupid concept, so go ahead and threaten. But no one, not one, on the outside, says a word. The silence is the honesty. So, when the spoken uses breath to make a listening, it is a hammer to the temple of the god of blonde brick entertainment patios. It's a *Saffir-simpson, category 5*, motherfucking Storm of catastrophic honest wordlessness, to the smiling man who signed the permit for the blasting of ancient ochre-painted messages to the future. Can he sleep? Will formaldehyde save his soul and be his resurrection?

How come *you* die then, when I won't. Don't? Can't? How come YOU don't bling the alleys with the kachinkachink long after your kids are dead? Because you're on the inside and the priests promised you immortality if you just whispered your sins after you turned five? Fuck me, they neglected to mention years in the nursing home. Antipsychotic calm. Tied to a chair to stop the running. They forgot to mention that raspberry flavoured, red jelly would mush your brain juices and reek the slick of your own destiny in the aftermath of thinking, *Hey! I'm somebody! See how well I did on the superannuation scheme? Wait... what?*

BRUISING

A back that is straight, and a woman who seethes with a hatred that makes no sense. No logical rationale. Because of her, a city is burning. People's hair is on fire. The wagons are filled with handcuffs made of yet more plastic. Cheap option, I guess, to iron ore and that old thing called a debtor's prison. Or the workhouse. Or *jack the ripper*. Oh, how we've evolved. And cops, so terrified that their jobs might turn out to be real police work, like protection and peace and all that dibdibdobdob stuff, that they wear black and blue like proud bruising. A threat. Walk bowed, you tattooed fucker! Walk bowed, you black bastard. Head down you piece of white trash. There's the gutter, motherfucker.

We walk tall.

Don't kid yourself for a minute there's no inside and outside cause

there is.

The dead didn't die, they just passed the Story to the living. It's a howl out here on the outside.

    HOWL

And the howl never concedes a *too late.*

Dirty, dusty rainswept, fearsomely-growing springtime morning, and wealth. Such wealth. That I have nothing for the woman in the bank. No smell, no social nicety, no hopeful reading of runes, or tarot, or ancestral song. It's the breath I breathe and, *An' I won't never need to be you*, relief, this smell of ozone and decay and ancient mother-milk that happens when land drinks from the sky.

And I hold the door handle. The key. But no, I need to bury it in its own rust. Give it to sister-sea, father-desert. It means nothing when it is out of a conscious person's grasp.

It could be thought to be rubbish or rubble but that's not true. Never could be. Nothing is wasted. That's not the meaning here. Despite the dereliction of what was once home. I understand rubble. I have something to build a Stonehenge with when I have sufficient rubble.

So... Just keep straight; walkin tall. Knowin the way home is way down, deep beneath the canopy some call skin. Where wild creatures mate and rear young. Where critters—called family—watch us, wary, because we haven't forgotten who is food. Eager, also, because neither have they.

Where wild creatures know a track, marked by stars, in patterns that streetlights try to blanket. That see through our eyes, where skin isn't.

Roaming without chains. Knowing home is *not* the house with the pool, surrounded by high fences but, *Oh, there's the view*. Safe distance. Security sensor lights. Stuff like that. We live in multiverses of critters. Archipelagos of reefs and shoals of infinitesimal birth-death-birth soup. Soughing Wind of lung and gut and sky. Bloody hands from pulling down the walls—illusions of condemnation and recrimination and resentment, oh, and fear—supposed to keep us from us.

Well, I'm outside. I kid you not. The being here is terrifying, but that's only the blade running down the length of deadwood, making a rhino in the whittling thereof. Remember them? For grandchildren. Tales of wonder. If I can keep this back straight, then the stories will be true.

As I told you once already, there is no *terra nullius*, child; children of us. Be quiet.

>You can hear the freedom.

...

DREAD AMONGST THE ROOTS

Firstly: I pay respect to the *Wurundjeri* and the *Boon Wurrung* people, and their elders past and present, in whose country I currently reside, and I dedicate this article to their knowledge and wisdom, and I acknowledge how staggeringly hard they are workin to educate us.

Secondly: This is not cheery rant. No. I'm whisperin on the wind to people of every species, from the left-over Treetops in the southlands, *Here: clear the undergrowth! Get ready for the big burn. In the Northlands, there: Stack the logs to the rafters, puppies, people gonna freeze four months from now.*

Is the above a prophesy? Yes. I will not insult you by suggestin why because, doubtless, we would not be chattin much at all unless being kindred creatures, under the same sky, giving thanks for the same rivers and lakes, and the same vastness of desert and curiosity, giving ceremony to the incalculable diversity of this here family-of-earth, as the seasons change us; call us to behave.

But I, doubtlessly like you, despise bullshit. And want to laugh at those in presumed authority that are hangin from the highest limbs of the human-branched tree, wieldin a chainsaw and tellin us we are safe because of them.

PART 1 – IDIOCRACY

About eight years ago I watched the movie *Idiocracy*. One of the people I gave birth to, now an adult (whatever that means) suggested it; said it was hilarious. The reaction I had to the film was similar to when I watched *The Truman Show*. Every blood vessel in this flesh-and-blood body slowed to an arctic, terrified, vortex-like freeze. They are not funny. They are even less so because they are happening.

So, I again sat immersed in *Koyaanisqatsi*, over and over, for several hours.

 COME ONE, COME ALL!

I have no doubt you all know there are—currently, obviously, gaudily, nauseatingly and glaringly—numerous conmen, strongmen, religious men, variations of Will Shakespeare's Complete Works or something, perhaps, from Poe. With an evangelical salt of earth, hatred-based ideology—pretty uniformly—based on a stupefying delusion, as they vie for prominence on a world stage, and jostle for a spotlight, dressed in suits and working the photo moments worse than *donald duck* ever could have envisaged, at the expense of incalculable life and life-sustenance. All of them in the flare of flashbulbs and, more alarmingly, at the dog's-lead-controlling end of the paper trail that leads to the anonymous, balaclava'd wielder of an AK 47, a pepper spray, a truncheon and a smoke-invasion of lachrymator. Or a bunch of tanks.

The 1993 *International Chemical Weapons Convention*, Geneva banned tear gas from being used where military forces are at war. However, a number of countries, including america, have approved its use of tear gas for *riot control* and for crowd control of non-military persons: theconversation.com.

Is it a fork on the track through the *Forêt Sauvage* of *Brocéliande*? No. And, sadly, there is not a single, lonesome grail castle to be found. The theatrics of attempted coercion, that of those in the glare of adulation, of the so-called *free west,* into a people of division and prolonged, contrived hierarchy, is becoming seemingly endless.

And we can't do it anymore. We have learned too much.

 PART 2 – TRACKS IN LONG GRASS

Grandchild starts high school in the year we condescendingly refer to as 2021 (apologies, to those of you who know we've got around 14 billion years under our atomic skin, whether that be as a procreative, multi-celled organism, or a vast flurry of interconnected electromagnetic snapshots and dark matter, hiding information that we, as a species, and for some undeniably hypothetically delusional seemingly-logical reason, has been taught to think of itself in terms as observational and ept) and they are working on a project to gain admission to the *cool kid* program of that institution. All those who aim for acceptance as some sort of pre-decided brightest, and referencing a lighthouse, are to present a unique angle, whereby they will pursue the creativity and research of this interest, particular to them, for between one and four years.

This child-adult relative has chosen to pitch a project that features indigenous methods and lore, featuring tattooing, body modification, and other essential cultural practices. Of course, I am heavily and intentionally inked, and identify as the direct descendant of Caradoc ap Cunobelin, by way of a matrilineal ancestry, a chieftain of the Catuvellaun people, a culture decimated but not eradicated, a memory and history that is woven intrinsically and irrevocably into the tapestry of seemingly endless invasions, and destruction of environment and culture, at the say-so of a fucken emperor on the take, no matter who gets killed or maimed, named *julius*, the harbinger of *claudius*—him and his war elephants—and a thousand years of usurpation.

Does anyone know the madness and murder associated with the so-called emperors of rome? The old-fashioned bureaucracy and hegemony responsible for the destruction of tribal Albion? Of the pogrom against Jerusalem and Nabataea that led to the hard right invention, by *paulists*, of a man-made sacrifice-on-a-cross bloke who allowed himself (in a flesh-and-blood *oopsie*, a chess-type-game certain man-made-gods occasionally play at to gain some kind of kudos, by infecting us with the guilt-fetish that somehow—like an alienly-introduced pox—seems built into the DNA of us hominids) to be tortured and mutilated—supposedly—in a ruse of lies and propaganda, that beg us to believe are necessary to eradicate the "sins of the world" (another *oopsie*; a twisted re-routing of crucifixion, a roman means of torture for sedition, into a one, man-made-god's gift, of letting us off the Eve-induced-*ereshkigal*-style meat hook, that *so* didn't work).

WHERE WAS I?

I put together a package for this grandchild: tattoo needles, gaffer tape and narrow wooden shafts with which to attach to the needles, ink, little plastic cups in which to hold that ink, gloves, pens, synthetic pigskin, spray bottle, sheets of wipes, and I forget what else. I mail it by express post. Along with a quick note warning that the ink is in a non-sterile container and therefore, if used on human animals, is likely to cause infection and possible death. Therefore, neutralizing a potential desire to ink his siblings, his mother, his friends, or the cat.

We arrange a Skype session, with no other purpose than that I bear witness to a first-ever attempt at tattoo. Their randomly-chosen design? A snake.

Why a snake? I ask.

Dunno... cause it's easy?

Not good enough.

Um, cause it means eternal life?

Are you kidding me?

They read somewhere, or heard tell of, an *ouroboros*-style ideology. I offer congratulations on having stolen an idea, but suggest it is a copout—an expected justification—to something perhaps more primitive, but profound, for all its animism. Tracks through long grass to the River, that includes the River in the tracking. This grandchild tilts their head, body language encouraging me to continue.

You know what happens when you go bush? I ask, knowing that a bunch of them—the family and many of their friends—go four wheel driving into remote areas regularly, where camp is set up and, come nightfall, they allow themselves to be crushed by the immensity of desert stars, and where calculating survival, from Land Rover to fresh water and back, takes strategy.

Yeah, why?

Do you ever walk though long grass to get from one place to another?

Yep.

In a line or all over the place?

I wait through the frown of remembering.

In a line. Always in a line.

How do you know to do that?

Never thought about it.

We don't, do we?

What?

Think about it. We just do it.

What's this got to do with the snake?

I'm possibly boring, with this line of interrogation, but I persevere. That's what grandparents do, by the way.

Well, it's possible that the person at the front of the line, or the person at the back of the line, is the most courageous of you all. If there're predators in the grass, I mean. First and last, eh? Who's gonna get bit?

Yeah, I get it.

And a river. Does a river go in a straight line?

Not that I know of.

Does a snake travel in a straight line?

Nope.

Could it be—a thought, maybe—that animals have traveled through

the long grass before you, to get to the water, and you're following where they've moved, since forever... and even if you can't smell 'em with a poor, archaic, almost-redundant scent ability, a bit of you knows there's actually is a track already?

That's possible.

Then, isn't it also possible that drawing a snake is like drawing a map?

Hey, that's cool.

TRUTH AND LIES

What is wrong with us? What have we become, as a species, that a virus (the harbinger of so much more) has to take us down? How must we listen and how must we bear witness, with full awareness, to the decimation of wetlands, the felling of forests, burning of vast tundras of grasslands and the plasticization of both the Arctic and Antarctic? Of the annihilation of insect species through the use of chlorpyrifos (let's not even mention *roundup, 245d & t*) and the outright stupidity of the need to decimate small species, deemed 'rodents' through the deadly and non-reversible use of 4-hydroxycoumarins, difenacoum, brodifacoum, difethialone, flocoumafen, and bromadiolone that, through the inevitability of the food chain, decimates the animal-people, of every variation, who get caught up in the chemical panic frenzy; who die relentlessly, because nobody spoke their language or put up an enormous billboard that reads DON'T EAT ANYTHING FOR THE NEXT 1,000 MILES?

> *If humans were to suddenly disappear, biologist Edward O. Wilson has famously observed, the Earth would "regenerate back to the rich state of equilibrium that existed 10,000 years ago." But "if insects were to vanish, the environment would collapse into chaos."*
>
> —National Geographic, May 2020.

Over the lintels of the *temple of apollo*, in Delphi, is the inscription *gnōthi seauton: know yourself*. It is followed by two other inscriptions: *nothing to excess* and *surety brings ruin*. And that last one is a doozy.

SURETY BRINGS RUIN

Surety brings ruin. What is that? Well, *diogenes* saw in it an expression of Greek philosophical scepticism, in other words, "Beware of committing yourself to false opinion" or "Beware false certainty."

We are aware, you and I, of the language of propaganda. I am, as you are, astonished that we are being presented with political, moral and ideological prattle, blather, balderdash and bullshit. Aren't I? Aren't you? What is the root of a tree but that which seeks the food from a vast and occulted environment, that is most nourishing; that teems with unrealized kindred, for tree-person as an entirety? That which supports, unseen, what is seen? What of us? As a species, we are hominids; the human expression of being. A single, self-reflecting creature, one of the plethoric, countless, kindred other self-aware beings that dance with mother earth. Do I include rock, wind, bacterium, salt, archipelago and puffer fish? Indeed. Yes, we think, and yes, we sometimes conclude that we are correct about some notion of freedom and equality and, even, the right to live with ancient lands and territories, unmolested and respected for no other reason than that we are creatures. Yes, we concur. Naïve stuff like that.

Until someone or something comes along, spreads the seeds of doubt, asks us (asks us?) to agree, or else machetes our children into bloodied pieces, burns down our homes, bombs the fuck out of our trade routes and allies, aerially pot shots freedom-herds of brumbies or buffalo, and then poisons waterways for a hundred thousand years because the technology is available *and, by god, we ought to be able to use this shit on somebody*! And pile us onto the backs of trucks to be lined up on the horizon of Maralinga or else stuffed into tower flats, called the most vulnerable in society, and imprisoned because... well...

> *Fear, anxiety, and, in some cases, anger characterised residents' responses. Worries about the risk of infection, mental health, nutrition, childcare, and access to medicine, services, and supplies were widespread. People resented the term "detention", especially given some residents' prior experiences in refugee camps and asylum seeker detention centres.*
>
> —Kaldor Centre, UNSW

...and placed under hard lockdown just to hint at what could possibly be consequential to objection (or sedition). Human animals, these laws and body-armour, go figure?

DOUBT SAP

Being acknowledged by the people that I pushed, living, from me, who are now adults, some of whom have also propagated and grown people from their bodies, is the same as our ancestors acknowledging the Pole Star as a god. As Navigator. As the time of year when this happens, or that happens, depending on Pole Star's positioning in a known, sung into future memory (needless of bookish authority) of this green or white or dark and moonlessly revered sky. I have purpose. You have purpose.

Sometimes, in what is known as "the Southern Hemisphere", life will journey into what is known as springtime. Native bees and European bees busy with pollinating. As are butterflies. And the poo of birds is dispersing seed far and wide (as is the springtime wind that people keep telling me is giving them the shits). Are they aware of what they do? Are we so *numpty* as to presume that this is their job? As though symbiosis is not a vast, reciprocal love? As though it were a chore, like accounting or doing one's tax?

What of honesty? What are we learning? What are we teaching kids?

What are we being told is the correct way to do anything? Why are we, currently, under the assault of men who proclaim themselves AS the Treetops while clutching to them in hope of not falling and becoming yesterday's news, wearing a versace suit and a fake tan? With a thought and a prayer; an ingratiatingly benign smile. With an anthem that demands: See me! See me, damn you! Me and my effing bible.

They are bulldozers, Critters. Our ancestors, however, and our future unborn children are along the Roots, within the Roots, and are fed by the sap of this awe-inspiring visceral body that knows what to do. Has always known what to do. Will, if left to procreate, always know what to do.

    FINGERS CROSSED NO LONGER WORKS

We are not stupid, and we do realize that the behavior of those who claim a spotlight, and who tell us what is best, and what the experts say, are lying. And that insects are disappearing, and birds are falling, dead, from the skies in north America. We do know that additives to food, poisons on the grain and salination of what has been, until recently (writing of the past 30 years only) life-sustaining, drinkable water, means some kind of unimaginable emptiness, eventually. And we are led to believe that, historically, this is what we do, as a species, and that we've always been this destructive. That it will *boost the economy* as though such a thing is a crippled, falling grandfather, once beaten into some unimaginable PTSD by a *"righteous"* war.

Question is, are we—human animals—all the same species? When what is being violated, in the name of righteousness, includes your children; your family, you, your mother, your culture and your humanity? Or are there potentially more than one hominid species and we just forgot about that? Or had the knowing intentionally removed from consciousness?

SNAKE WITH NO NAME

And then, after all this, can we ask why Snake-Person, about to be inked into memory, is not enough? Why snake has to be other? Why snake-person is deemed evil? A temptation of the weaker sex? Dangerous, and therefore, expendable? Wicked, or symbolic of eternal life? Like sharks and tigers; that one final white rhinoceros? That mother orangutan standing defiantly before the bulldozer.

PART 3 – I AM THE STORM

Are you still going to tattoo the snake?

Yes.

If you're asked by the teachers why you chose em, what'll you say?

I'll think of something.

I laugh. The drawing starts. Then the tattooing. A mess. For a couple of minutes. Until the hang of it is achieved. The completion of the ink-snake takes about an hour. And, at that completion, grandchild-person is rather chuffed. But realize this:

Between our first conversation, and the presentation the day after the use of the tattoo needle, this eleven year old human being has watched every episode of *Skindigenous*, has researched *ta moko* and the traditions of the islanders of the South Pacific. He has also begun to explore this country's First Nation people's tradition of scarification to mark their initiated, instead of ink (or else unknown to us palefaces); the learning of law and lore—

> *Traditionally in Indigenous Australian culture, scarification was a signifier of a person's place in the community and an expression of identity, experience and beauty— almost a non-verbal language carved right onto the skin*
>
> —Michael Jalaru Torres, Scar III

Are you in?

I got the first place, he tells me. Not proudly, not cocky, just matter-of-factly, like they knew it would happen.

NOW

Again, the seasons turn. Yes. And closer to the Arctic we are in the chill of autumn, and the air is already hinting at unprecedented snow (like we thought the last year's was). And I'm still in woollies, with the hearth fire on. We are the People of the South, yet those of us with pale skin are new, and need elders, other hominids like us, but attuned to rock and cloud and wallaby and tawny frogmouth and the news that insect people know because they have been here since before Gondwana. The freshly-dead whales are a warning, and despite the few who listen to their story, before they expose us to consequence, are horrified by what they conclude.

Today I sent word to human-kin, in other parts of this continent, that mother-landscape is going to burn. Those swinging from the branches of what remains of the forests giants and great ferns, are still posturing. They did NOT listen to the First Nation People's wisdom of controlled fire. Did NOT sit at the feet of knowledge-holders to learn understanding and respect for the land and waters. Utter violation, that's again and still, the contempt. Yet, you and I can bend the knee and move out of the way. We are the magic people. It's time for the next great revolution. It will not be fought with guns and bombs.

It will not be fought at all. Silence will be the most terrifying outcome. People of the North listen to the elders. Have an alternative to electricity. Don't be afraid. Be the next hundred years.

The coming storm is going to be epic.

...

THE HUNTER, I
(Explained)

PART 1—An Mhaighdéan Mhara

This story is conjured from the contemplation of many myths surrounding what is accepted as legends of selkies. Women (usually) who come ashore, remove their skins and are captured by human men, their skins hidden.

While I can see the symbolic idea of losing one's identity to bureaucracy, propaganda, sale, disillusionment, rape, marriage, religiously deliberate expedience, confiscation and—sometimes—obliteration of individuality, I also propose, as in the story of Snow White actually representing the travel of salt along the Rhine, and the anthropomorphic tales that, for children, are the process of learning, simplistically, about cultural history and decimation, and knowing that as they become wise and grow, as per all other indigenous cultures, in the way of elders, that sourcing the stories is what lies beneath.

We, as a pale people, have not kept ourselves to this process of progressive initiation, hence wisdom and connection to land, season, ancestors and customs have been, to a large extent, buried (I will not say lost as that implies a lie).

The first story, An Mhaighdéan Mhara *(The Sea Maiden)*, is a contemporary selkie tale.

The second, The Hunter I *is drawn from the crevasses of imagination, summoned along the blockchain of an immortal DNA, but I have researched myth and folktale sufficiently, however, to want to speak to you in their voices. Therefore, these legends, although spread thinly amongst scholars and students of Celtic and Gaelic lore (including druidry) are probably based on a living and important event that is, or has been, buried deep within this DNA. Of course, as with most data, it is uncoverable and accessible.*
This is not so much to convince the reader as to raise questions regarding what we understand as folklore and folk tales. Perhaps they are much, much more.

Perhaps, as a result of a condescending conqueror, they have been made childlike and considered inconsequential; nothing more than frippery.

We offer this as the beginning of a conversation and a hunt for authenticity.

AN MHAIGHDEÁN MHARA

He sat on the closest rock, with the cold black water and her lace-like froth shushing at his edges, his boots, his tiny rubber currach held onto, without thinking, by its rope. He watched me with some emotion, some edges of both passion and panic that made no sense to me yet, with eyes that were the dark brown of a distant relative and that told me of his soul. *Alright,* I thought at him. *I'll play with you, I have to, so do not look away.*

And he did not. He heard me thinking.

I was slow for him, reaching up and pulling my face away. That first rush of air on my other skin caught my breath and it was I, not he, who shuddered with surprise. He did not drop his gaze from mine even then, as if to say, *I'm with you, do not be afraid.* I give love for that, for he should have been in dread if the stories were true.

Down my neck I rolled it, over one shoulder, slid along the other, pulled it to below both breasts, enticing. His eyes widened and his nostrils did this little thing, and I knew why. He looked upon the milk white skin of a woman wherever the silk of my silver pelt peeled away. He breathed faster, because he knew what I was and what I could do and what was to come and what I would give, and that I would leave him. And all of it I read in his eyes, with their deep black centers that grew wider with each breath until the rim had all but been pushed aside.

No one he knew had ever seen this, he told me later, only spoke of it as though it might just have once been real, him covering my freezing flesh with his arms, knowing my pelt would soon consign the chill into memory, what a gentle man he turned out to be. How could I have resisted?

He'd anchored himself, against some legendary seventh wave, in those great boots, that thick woolen jacket covered by a sou'wester that stood out like a sail in the wind, smelling of the fish of days gone by, his jeans filthy where he'd rubbed his hands on them after gutting.

He dropped the rope.

In confusion I comprehended that it was me who could not look away. We'd fished this same wild sea garden for generations, and we'd seen each other a hundred times or perhaps a hundred more and we had so much love to give each other, and I was ripe, and I didn't question that it was to be him.

Down, down over my hips and knees. And not even to kill him or to do any of the things my mother and her mother had told me that I could do. And why would I? No, just to lie with him and love.

I step from one skin only to expose another, all the way, and let it go, as though of little consequence. His eyes wander my nakedness before I take hold of him, touch his roughness, and pull him further from the water.

You just going to leave it? he whispered, as he fumbled his gloves off and reached around my shoulders with his salt stiff jacketed arms, but with hands as careful as could be. As if it my true self would go off on its own. Why would he think that? And there was no one else and the cliff was his.
I knew the stories, so I had no fear. We followed the grooves in the sand, into the little shelter that kept the wind away and that stank of things I would never need the words for. He laid me down on his big woolen coat and kissed my lips. He explored my woman body and then he entered me and oh, this was what a man was and what he did, and what a woman could feel, and it was wordless, absolutely wordless.

He wrapped me in the coat, and we lay together with just the sound of the wind and the sea and the gulls up on the cliffs. And then I sighed and stood and pulled him, frowning, from the floor and he was sad. But I could never have stayed.

And unlike the other stories he walked me to the water's edge, took back his coat, and watched, and shivered and cried just a little, as I stepped into my skin.

I took to the black water, his child within me, and I saw him every day that he came.

We shared that same wild sea garden as long as he was alive. And he knew.

THE HUNTER, I

1.

This Hunter, that is I, sits at the central fire, head bowed, seems to sleep. Is listening. Is breathing deeply of rock and tree people, mist-wet hair and fur, breast milk and boar upon coals, the metallic tang of torc, bog water and loam, old sap bled from broken branches. That storm. That death storm to be remembered. Hunter, I, searching out rhythm. Distant carrion smell of newly dead, bones not yet picked quite by eagle and crow and wolf pack. This hunter, I, knows all this.
It's in the memory of muscle and the story of lore. And the children watch, those that can stay awake this deep into the long night, as one by one and two by two the others come, silently and frost-breathedly, for what? A new walk? No such thing. The walk of the ancestors who are gone, then?

Yes, a song the elders have remembered, and tell every word the song like a heartbeat. The song of a bright-faced hunter, that one, just one hunter, who called softly to her mother, her name and her purpose -to just once follow the *reinsdyr* and so learn where they go for the long dark. Of her twin who had gone also. Who never returned. Such a story!

And babies sleeping upon the backs of the ones who will stay (because it's not their time).

This Hunter, I, who is to walk towards the silent, ever-moving color-wind, and the star that nails the world to the sky. Green and green, arching and twisting in an erotic, threatening show of power. Nor'-east is this name. Beyond the black earth. Beyond the rock of summer coast where the mackerel last spawned.

Before the ice-night slept the otter, and the *uruz* cracked the last of the big lake's possible fishing, and we watched them running down the sun, oh two, three moons withstanding snow beyond the seas of *reinsdyr*, warner of the first big ice, and, cousins-mine, the white wolf hunters and bear-to-sleeping. To follow the memory of whale-blow, the ancestor spring-thaw song.

To never neglect the land-knowing that must be seen. Or perish.

Without this must-know-but-don't-remember-why story, we, the People, will end this being now.

Drummers gather. And the old people, the keepers of all lore, singers
of the first day. This hunter, I, and the others who are now many, dance. Fur-thick, feather-haired, bird-boned and, old woman hunter, I, walrus-tooth-hung, we dance warm-blooded other people, and we dance *shark,* and we dance *spear magic*. Hunter magic. Birdcall magic and ice-to-stay-strong magic. And singers sing: white bird, forever shark and break-the-ice-but-not-fall-in-magic. All night, which is every night and every day, until no one knows anything else except warm-blooded, white bird and forever shark. Warm-blooded, forever shark... and seal magic. Yes. Seal magic to remember who we remember but don't know why. Just in case we meet them again. Being impolite is not a hunter, I, a hunter way.

Then Hunter, I, and the others who are now many, walk into the land beyond the story because everyone, although they sing, and rock the children and beat the drum, is silent with hunger so someone must add to the story. That is us.

And the People we leave behind, in the night between night and day, cry to remember us, for if we are ancestors, and not returners with food, they will care for our children and they will howl before they become meat for cousins, bear and howler wolf, cousins big white crab and slow melt for slow shark... for love of us.

Thus Hunter, I, and the others, travel the winter's end thunder road that moves towards what will be the later spring shoreline after the melt, towards way, way deep into the path of dawn-rise. A girdle of land, ice-no-melt we hope, that will not end until we reach beyond the world. Into the endless sea. And it is a long, long road.

2.

Biggest seals ever in our stories we see now. Swim between the ice flows with white grey whales. Most peculiar, hunter, I, decide. Seals within seals like a many-breasted woman bearing her babies on her belly, moves through the water. Paddles like feet. Duck-seals.
Hoy! Hoy! Heya! They cry, like people, standing on two legs and waving spears pointed towards sky and not at us. Hunter, I, and the others, not so. Feed the People waiting in the long dark, by the quiet fires, when? Half a sky round ago. Half a moon ago.

Hoya, hey! They yell, laughing and rhythm-banging on the flank of mother seal, she not slowing her swimming through the black, deep waters, between the ice flows, with white grey whales passing us by, but them not.

Hoy! Hoy! Hunter! Calls and calls as they come close and we ready to harpoon. *Don't hurt us, we are returning to the People!*

And I, Hunter, I and others all around me hear the ice crack and the whales *tewel* to each other as they dive and breach and dive and breach. So long do we not say a word or even hear our breathing over the drumsong of this heartbeat, saying who, who? Who, who? What is this story? We, all hunters us, be very, very quiet, and disregard nothing, for magic is not predictable. And this is not predictable. That the seal says *hoya, hey* and laughs... is not predictable.

Not a seal. Neither a mother seal nor any other seal. But the skins of many, sewn about the bone of otherkin. floating like an ice flow but faster. Seals but not seals. People in the skins of seals, harpooning the frozen earth, mooring rope upon the frozen earth, one stepping from the barge with great height and light eyes and smiling teeth and wide-open arms. And hunter, I, am in those arms as warm as flesh that has sat beside the fire, that has rolled in furs for pleasure, and from such as this the babies sometimes come.

This face is the same as a brother and a mother, but it is not their face.

3.

The people of the seal have come home. And the hunting magic rights the hunger. And the people of the seal bring stories of another place,
where they have lived with other people, people that they love as they love us. To whom they will return.

They sing the place they have found. Down the river of the sun. The way of the boats they have learned to make, to cross the wide, dark sea. They sing the name of the bright-faced person, that one, just one hunter, who called softly to her mother, her name and her purpose—to just once follow the *reinsdyr* and so learn where they go for the long dark. Of her twin who accompanied her. Of what they found. Of a land of fire mountains and of thunder underfoot. Another People. All in the long ago. All still here.

Will you stay?
No. But we will lie amongst your furs for the remainder of the long dark, and roll with you, and so perhaps take babies when we go. The children of the seal are we.

Will they be?

Just as you, hunter you, are daughter of the white wolf, and that person walking with that drum is the caller to the thunder, and the hunting magic. Just as she, over by the river's new Dancer, is the eagle-whisperer, and he is the maker of things of fine-honed bone harpoon. We will love you until the uruz return to the valley.

Until the white grey whale fills the now-pale sky-silver sea with their young as they travel the ways of their ancestors, to the southern other. When the silent, ever-moving color-wind fades to sleeping, and the star that nails the world to the sky shows us that summer will soon bring the otter and the mackerel... and the mosquitoes... we will go.

And we will teach you the songs that we know! We will teach them for all of these days. Oh, that is exciting says the keeper of the lore, joining I, the hunter and the something else, yet to be. Yet to be.

To make the seal boat? I? I have spoken aloud what has been only in dream. I have dared ask this magic...I will take the sea road of the bright-faced person. One day, I will take the sea road, yes?
Yes. To make the seal boat and take the sea road, yes.

And the way to come to you? The stars to come to the land of the fire mountain?
Yes.

Will the others, who are not us, not kill us?
No. They are us, also.

Then I, Hunter I, I will learn the way to come to you!
The way to come to us and the stars that will lead you to our children.

Our children?
Yes, our children.

...

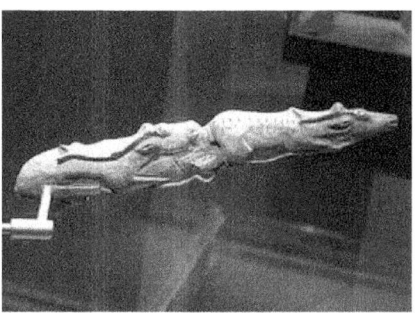

Image Swimming Reindeer

The Swimming Reindeer is the name given to a 13,000-year-old Magdalenian sculpture of two swimming reindeer conserved in the British Museum. The sculpture was made in what is now modern-day France by an unknown artist who carved the artwork from the tip of a mammoth tusk. The sculpture was found in two pieces in 1866, but it was not until the early 20th century that Abbé Henri Breuil realized that the two pieces fit together to form a single sculpture of two reindeer swimming nose-to-tail.

[1] The celestial North Pole moves in a circle around the center point, which is situated in the Draco constellation. One round takes 25,770 years and the mechanism causing this movement is precession, the slow movement of the axis of rotation in a gyroscope. In the case of the Earth this movement is for unknown reasons called precession of equinoxes. Equinox is a time: a day when the day and night are of equal length. Equinox changes because of precession, but the movement would be more logically called precession of the Earth axis. Already 1983 Ugo de Santillana and Ertha Von Dechend argued in that all ancient cultures knew the precession of equinoxes.

...

A TAD OF RAPTURE

Last night I sat, unmoving (spring possums...you know it, here in Melbourne, or autumn bats, like lightning shadows, in Arizona and Dublin) in this recently winter-woke garden, with the sudden, unbidden realization that I see better in the dark than I do in daylight (I wear glasses in daylight). So, understandably, I wonder about us as a species. Do we adapt when we think? Is there even an *us*, when, really, we are a composite of trillions of years of birth, death, compost and regeneration? Of *She* who held us—future ratbags—in her eggs, and her mother, in hers?

This same night brother wind blows oh, what? countless keratinocytes off face and hands. The only bits of me exposed. It's still cardie and scarf weather here. I haven't EVER thought about this before. That in any day we shed a good million of these—

> *Keratinocytes are formed at the base of the epidermis, and gradually move up through the skin until they reach the outer surface, where they die, forming the stratum corneum, somewhat around 15-20 layers of dead cells. Eventually, the critters at the very surface break away and fall off, allowing new cells to push up from beneath. This is the natural life cycle of the skin.*

Thought meanders to icebergs (just finished reading *Underland*, and the writer, Robert Macfarlane, is a blanket who has wrapped me in a newly spun tapestry of sighs and breaths and mumbles). You know icebergs *calve*? The outer edge shears off and merges with mother-ocean, kind of like being born. Do you know the sun does something similar? That spent and decaying sunspots are transported from her surface to her poles, where she drags them, like unschooled puppies, into her heart, to regenerate them and give them another chance at

surface-swelling again... and again, and again.

Then, and this is the interesting bit, as the countless spent skin cells blow away, I wonder if that's what happens to the whole of the *me* that I think of as me? If I'm slowly disintegrating. That if any of us live long enough, we develop valleys and canyons, dinosaur-skinned dunes, and sinkholes, where the bits blow away, are eaten by the landscape or collapse in preparation for a new season or being?

That's interesting, isn't it? We don't think of breezes as powerful. Rain and washing water as razor blades and cheese cutters. But, like the nuns say, of time in their perversely-invented hell, things change one sparrow-peck of the mountain at a time.

We could be said to melt. Shaped by season and circumstance into individual earths. Sculpted.

Liberation, that is. To alter the perception of aging from something the cosmetic industry deludes us into thinking is an abomination, to some wondrous wilderness of susurrating breaths, feeding trees with each expiration, river-valley fjord, face and belly folds and lace-like, bird-thin, holy bones. Somewhat light, like pumice from spent volcanic passion. Able, in a mere 40,000 years, to remain as rubble, to remind a vast herd of unborn grandchildren of who they truly are? If homo-erectus is even our destiny, or some delusion of species naming for some hope of importance.

Image: Newgrange, Ireland

Perspective.

That's for tonight.

A night-sight chance to touch outmoded understanding...

With oh, yes, that exquisite tad of rapture.

...

ROADKILL IN A ONCE-UPON-A-TIME-FOREST

What—or who—defines reality? Does the discussion of an unexplored thing—the naming, temporarily—of that thing, make it real? Once we've named it, however, it belongs to us, does it not? It becomes familiar.

Oh, yes, that's right... We can discuss it, kill it, dissect it, love it, adore it, destroy it, abandon it, dress it up, forget about it, understand it, hate it, question it, make it fit, describe it to others, teach about it, be in charge of it, wear it, treat it, vaccinate against it, wage war over it, seduce it or eat it. I'm sure you can expand on the list.

I'm on track but that does not denote a bitumen road rendering a once deer-and-wolf-abounding forest in half, so that people, in their righteousness, can comment, Slow down! Roadkill! When it's the road that kills by slicing the forest in two, and we agree by driving along it.

So. Real. It is written somewhere, "naming is treacherous because naming divides truths into half-truths, making a coffin of counters... be careful... give the spell no name."

As for *witchcraft*? Some people have been in the scene and have walked away. But was that *witch* they were disillusioned by or what was presented in the name of *witch*? I suggest the latter... The titling of *witch* was, once upon a time, sufficient to get a woman killed. Men were not murdered, generally, for the accusation of witchcraft. No. They would have died, like Giordano Bruno, for being heretics. Even *coven*—the word—simply implies a gathering. Nothing inherently to do with witchcraft (except here, and just now). Witch is druid (druí), if one is a Celt. It is *noadi* if you are trained as such, it is other if you are.

Let's for a moment look at the *ness* of things and see what this implies, even after I have sought and presented you with *Snow White* (salt or
springtime) and the preposterous notion of *fairy story*, let alone one or the kiddies...

Witch scares people. The word sends a shiver down the spine. No matter who you are, in the background of your stored learning is the idea of evil. Of sex with the devil. But also, the lore that not everything is as it seems and that some things are unknown... discussed through a tainted and biased lens. That we can name the thing that lurks behind you. That curses can be cursed, that goblins steal newborn children or that sorcery can dry up milk of cattle.

When one thinks of the practitioners of witchcraft one sees potentially several things, depending on one's proclivity and place in the world.

Image: Pinterest: The Craft (1996)

Silly: pointy black hats and green faces riding broomsticks across a full moon night sky.

Frightening: women on the floor in chalk-drawn pentagrams lighting candles and whispering incantations.

Storybook: old hags living alone in cottages in the woods burning children in ovens.

Bigoted: tribal men or women in west Africa slitting the throats of goats.

Quaint: silver-haired matrons in lavender gardens with rabbits around their feet.

Movie-style: teenage girls in black lipstick with layers of rosary beads and silver pentagram jewelry around their necks, usually in threes, often with a pretty blonde Anglo European good girl whose destiny is to be, unsurprisingly, the most powerful.

Secretive: indistinguishably-gendered, cloaked and hooded people in a circle. Darkened room or crypt with altars, chalices and arcane symbols, summoning demons to destroy the world.

Wiccan: robed, adult flower children with ornate staffs or daggers, looking skyward with their arms open wide, in all seriousness, invoking, summoning, beseeching, drawing down, moting or blessing, in the names of usually Celtic, European or Levantine supreme beings, not as important as the christian god but necessarily worshipped in quantities because, dammit, they were cast aside and now must save a doomed world or heal a terminally ill individual.

Where was I going with this? Oh yes. How people deal with fear.

    DEALING WITH FEAR = DELUSION

They buy the products that sell online and in little stores. They attend the workshops and fulfill the criteria of 'witch schools'. All for a price. Hey, a girl's got to make a living and it's better than shelf-stackin in a supermarket.

That's lowbrow, though, isn't it? Highbrow is anthropology or archaeology. It's also Jungian psychology or, gag, Freudian (do they even do that blame and transference shit anymore). Stuff one has to achieve a university-accredited set of letters to proclaim. Sometimes a good excuse to live amongst indigenous people and explore their super-good hallucinogenic medicine. Even me, writing another book and calling it *A Witch's Guide* to blah blah. It's all still colonialism suggesting a 'better than' approach to otherness.

And exploration? *Darkest* Africa. Castles lined and adorned with the trophies of the intrepid *massah* in his pith helmet. Atop elephants scouring India for gemstones. Robbing graves, desecrating rainforest canopies, condemning free people to enslavement, sailing them to death or entrapment, to America, the Caribbean, Australia... oh everywhere the empire wanted, if we're honest. What is real? And why do we agree to anything? An elf is a little creature? A fairy is a little winged figure in the bottom of the garden? Witches aren't real?

BLAME

What are people teaching children? That lies are an acceptable means of communication? Yes. When children are taught, in christian households, that a man died a cruel death nailed to a cross of wood 2000 years ago, based on zero evidence, thrust into a hill named *golgotha* formed of stone. Not only that but it is said to be within the private property, a thing that was against Roman law as the spectacle of consequence to insurgency was meant to be a public warning, and the supposedly *messianic* figure recounted as strung up between two thieves, also crucified... ow are these myths acceptable as they are without reference to social mores? In difference to the lore of other cultures?

When the history is explored it is found that Jewish autocracy, under roman jurisdiction, could sentence people for several crimes, one of which was theft, but that the cutting off of a hand, or public flogging was the norm, never crucifixion. That was reserved for sedition, by Rome, against Rome. So, the tale of the thieves is laughable. As is the entire fable when examined under the microscope of occidental mythology. It has even been suggested by scholars that the attributes and acceptable debasements in that religion were created by rome as a way of indoctrinating a caste to servitude. (Sources for these theories are from books read in the 1990s, references not kept). If we consider these themes of malice and intentional slaughter, in relation
to the crusades—over two hundred years in duration—what we encounter is a pointless human relationship to death... but not necessarily an animist one. So that children, said to be taught a truth are, instead, reduced to indoctrination and confusion.

THE CRUSADES—HOLY GRAILS AND THE LAND GRAB

The campaigns, to regain a formerly annexed property of the roman empire, commenced in 1095 and ended in 1291, and there were nine crusades in all. Records of events were maintained only until the end of the third crusade. The exact number of people leaving home on this pointless journey were never recorded, the exception being kings and knights who took along not just the warriors, but servants, wives, and others not actively involved in the *crusade*.

What historians agree on is that many so-called Anglo-Saxon *nobles* returned to their territories after the stint in this useless experience of slaughter, starvation and bloodshed, only to find their once tribal, territories and estates occupied by Normans, their names and titles taken, identities almost extinguished, sanctioned by the papacy and enforced by his agencies. Hence the stories of *Robin O'Hood*.

Considering all this impotence, and the establishment of a hard core, right wing, militant religious government it is not surprising that a modicum of royal-house arse-licking ensued. That is still happening, but it was at a propaganda peak throughout Europe and England during the years of the Inquisition, beginning around 1250 and is in existence today, although quite covert; known as *the sacred congregation for the doctrine of the faith* and, amongst laity, *opus dei*.

JUST A FEW? PLAGUE, THE ONE-ONLY LIE

—1st PANDEMIC (*The Plague of Justinian*) circa 500 – 554 CE

This plague (bubonic, it is assumed) was attributed to an emperor named *Justinian*, and it is alleged to have begun at Constantinople and to have spread to the Mediterranean district: Who records this? Procopius, a Greek scholar of the era writes in his work *Secret History*, that Justinian was a demon of an emperor who either created the plague himself or was being punished for his sinfulness. Justinian, while considering himself a christian, was branded a heretic by the *council of chalcedon*, and labeled a *monophyte*. Heaps of trade, heaps of war, masses of travel although not by him. Estimated deaths 25 to 50 million but I ask myself, who comes to this figure? Who thinks of this? How do they know?

—2nd PANDEMIC (*black death*) circa 1347 to 1352 CE

Not only textbooks, but serious monographs on the *Black Death* and its successive waves of plague into the early 19th century in Europe, go on about rats (usually the black ones) and fleas without qualification. But what is the evidence? No contemporary observers described any epizootic (animal epidemic) of rats or of any other rodents immediately before or during the *Black Death*, or during any later plagues in Europe as relevant or specific—that is, until the 'third pandemic' at the end of the 19th century.

Some of the worst-hit regions were in mountainous and relatively isolated zones, such as in Snowdonia in wales or the mountain village of Mangona, north of Florence, whose communications with the wider world were less frequent than places further down the slopes and closer to cities. The experiences of these isolated villages may have been similar to small mining villages in Pennsylvania or in south Africa, or Inuit settlements in Newfoundland under attack in New York city or London.

In German-speaking lands, France along the Rhine, and parts of Spain, municipal governments, castellans, bishops, and the *holy roman emperor* accused Jews of spreading the *black death* through poisoning foodstuffs and water sources. The papal army massacred entire communities of women, men, babies, elders, kindred animals for
these supposed crimes. The accusations and atrocities, however, were not universal between 1348 and 1351. Although *the Pied Piper* cites 1376 as a pretty fucked year for a Jewish diaspora, apparently in Hungary [1]. Massacres did not arise in the British Isles (where, at least in England, Jews had been expelled in 1290, by edward I), and no clear evidence pinpoints any such violence in Italy (except for the Catalans in Sicily). Nor are any mass annihilations, of human animals that is, recorded in the middle east.

—3rd PANDEMIC: 19th century

Associated with china and spread as far as Chinatown in San Francisco. Rodents may not have been connected to any of this as is popularly attributed. We could also be looking at either smallpox as was introduced to indigenous populations to wipe them out, or early *ebola*, or even forms of streptococcal outbreak. Who knows? We still have *ringa roses* though. Without questioning, usually, why we teach this to children.

There has never been a period throughout recorded history without a plague. Yersinia. Pestis. Bubonic, Septicaemic and/or Pneumonic. Not endemic in Australia but is widely distributed around the world [2]. The W.H.O reports 1,000 to 3,000 cases of plague EVERY YEAR. Plague is endemic in some parts of south-east Asia, including parts of Indonesia, Burma and Vietnam. Wild rodent plague exists in areas of the united states of America, south America, Africa and central and south-east Asia.

Untreated bubonic plague has a case-fatality rate of about 50–60 per cent. Case-fatality rates are significantly higher for pneumonic and septicemia plague.

Given that techniques for mass production and aerosol dissemination are well described, the threat of a bioterrorist attack using plague is a potential public health concern.

FOLK TALE—THE PIED PIPER

The *malleus* elevates sorcery to the criminal status of heresy and prescribes inquisitorial practices for secular courts in order to extirpate people it deemed *witches*. The recommended procedures include torture, to effectively obtain confessions, and the death penalty as the only sure remedy against the evils of what it deemed consorting with demons and the christian devils. At that time, it was typical to burn those accused alive. The book had a strong influence on human behavior, belief and fearmongering, for several centuries.

While the official church doctrine stated that there was no such thing as witchcraft, and the construct widely agreed upon, demonic possession was attributed to everything from epilepsy to the effects of ergot, a fungus that grew on rye in marshy environments (basis for LSD). The church did, after all, create an exorcism ritual to torment the sick. What is little known is the scandalous acquisition of property that occurred throughout these frenzied years, right into the 17th century in Scotland, whereby a *witch-dobber* was awarded a percentage of the condemned person's property, while the church acquired the majority.

VERONICA FRANCO

The Italian pandemic of 1629–31 was a series of outbreaks of possible bubonic plague which ravaged northern and central Italy. This epidemic, often referred to as the *great plague of Milan*, is estimated to have claimed possibly one million lives, or about 25% of the population.

Before this, however, in 1575 during yet another record of plague, Veronica Franco, a courtesan of vast wealth and learning was forced to leave Venice. Much of her booty was looted and her house and possessions decimated. On her return in 1577 christian authorities alleged that *her witchcraft* actually caused the plague. She was charged, imprisoned and eventually brought before the inquisitional judges. With recommendations she be burned to death. She was acquitted. On evidence from her sexual allies, among the venetian nobility, including the very catholic *doge* of Venice. Her later life is largely obscure, and although her fate is uncertain, she is believed to have died in relative poverty. Like most women historically uppity.

In *Britain*, which by this era includes Scotland [3], the *Scottish witchcraft act* was established, in 1563 whereby both the practice of witchcraft and consulting with witches were capital offences, and in 1604, the year following james' accession to the English throne, the *elizabethan act* was broadened to include the death penalty without benefit of clergy, to anyone thought to invoke a devil, or commune with familiar spirits. The *act's* full title was *An Act against Conjuration, Witchcraft and Dealing with Evil and Wicked Spirits*. It was this statute that was enforced by matthew hopkins, the self-styled *witch-finder general*.

Through the 1640s the *general assembly of the church of Scotland*, and the *commission of the kirk,* lobbied for the escalation and extension of the *witchcraft act* 1563, and the hunting and killing of *witches*. The regime passed a series of laws, enforcing *godliness,* which made capital offences of blasphemy, the worship of false gods and for beaters and cursers of their parents. This act was not repealed until 1951, and in queensland, sometime in the 1980s. In many lands and cultures murder is still perpetrated for
the practice of cultural wisdom.

21st CENTURY AND—

So now I come to the gathering of stories and lore. Of so-called folk tales, later malformed into the twisted indigenous defamation of fair-folk stories, made popular by the *grimm brothers* and, in our centuries: 20th and 21st, of the *common era*, by *little golden books, disney, walmart, kmart* or *7-eleven*, near the lolly counter.

In 1812, the first published copy of jacob and wilhelm grimms' collection of gathered and interpreted folk tales was published. From where, and from whom, did the brothers gather these tales? Supposedly told them by word of mouth, throughout a thoroughly terrorized, christianised and also, by now, utterly *dark-aged* population of Europe that had learned to keep its mouth shut? D'you think, for one moment, that indigenous mysteries, of a romanticized origin, were part of those stories? That these dandies in suits, fresh from university, were going to *Monty Python* it into remote Carpathian villages and request a meeting with the local, surviving and admitted soothsayer, who would gladly disclose to them the legends and lore of a non-christian ancestor, thoroughly wise, who had kept hold, unpolluted, tales of profundity? That these now thoroughly flattened, drunken and plague-poxed leftovers of a proud Celtic, Gallic, Saxon and non-christian heritage knew the lore of princesses and queens with magic mirrors? Hmm?

Had some obscure byzantine seeress or wizard, stopped by one afternoon, desperate for a bed for the night and fodder for their exhausted horse, and paid for it with a tale of dwarves and glass coffins?

What, then, if anything, are these stories? And why do we subject them to children? The so-called *queen* who wanted Snowy dead was first published as her mum, in 1812, who disliked her daughter's challenging beauty and requested she be butchered in a nearby forest, her liver and lungs delivered to the dinner table. Not a *step-*mother. Not a *mother* at all. That had to wait until the outcry, like what happened to Freud. Someone had the brothers rewrite the story, inventing the death of Snow's biological mother at her daughter's birth, and the instatement of daddy's new wife, called variously *stepmother* or *evil queen* and considered a narcissist, and delivered into history as the true nature of any woman who dares usurp a loving mummy.

What *is* all this? An *evil queen*? Sending a little girl off to be murdered when she was seven years old (as odd as the fallacy of an old fat man
being allowed to slip, silently, into a child's bedroom at night, without adult supervision, and providing gifts, if said child has been a good little kiddie... by someone, anonymous, with standards of goodness of which we know nothing)?

What was that story about? The idea of the mirror? The mother sending her daughter to the slaughter? The wolf as the bad guy who kills children and not bunnies? The woman preparing to cook children in her oven in the woods? The woman, not invited to the christening, cursing the girl to grow up and sleep forever unless some man wakes her with a non—consensual pash-up? The dwarfs that in the original story (who had no names but represented 7 mountains) somehow acquiring a glass or crystal coffin in which to store the undead body. Those anonymous small people selling the seemingly-dead girl—of purportedly, now, marriageable age—to some random traveling nobleman with enough moolah to purchase a glassed-in human being? That display case made of glass, when glass hardly existed let alone be known about to the story-telling peasant Jacob and Wilhelm allegedly visited.

It was shattered, by the way, by disgruntled servants sick and tired of carrying the object from room to room for the *nobleman* to admire has he attended to his affairs. They dropped it, smashing the container, on purpose (and nope, no prince woke her), by the way, the fall dislodging a chunk of apple, not poisoned, that was stuck in her throat, like an unheard protest at entrapment, disgorged when she fell. You see there is something enforced going on. Some acquiescence to privilege. People calling daughters, or granddaughters little princesses, dooming them to the reality of both perennial adult-lying and the disillusionment of being just nobody in particular.

The *squander fest* around *christmas*, that I am fed by every so-called *witch* or *pagan* who claims that it's all about family when family is there 364 other days of the year. The word *fairy* being a painted, diminutive, winged creature.

Human consciousness has acquired an imagination for the fantastic. I have no grievance about story. A cracking tale, like any exquisite art, is a force of nature. It's the pretend it's real when it should be pretend that I find cruel. Until we can admit that we should not be building that road and until we claim culpability in our deceit, we are complicit.

We live in a sliver of a season within which we can challenge paradigms that celts were/are headhunters... well, even that we were and not are... when it was Europeans taught the Indians to scalp the dead, and Europeans that cut off the hands of Africans and chained First Nation people, and that *pagan* is a latin word that comes from the language of a conquering hegemony, that *gods* and *goddesses* are anthropomorphic people-modeled reflections of ourselves... oh... nothing to do with the living earth...

Until we do, and while we sell or buy dream catchers, misappropriate the lore of others maimed by usurping and colonizing hegemonies, until we question the very essence of childhood and our part in a travesty of lies, we are part of a collective delusion and we cannot recover.

Because we are still outlaws...

SQUARE: *Credit card facilities: "Your account is canceled!"*

    Terms & Conditions:

By creating a Square Account, you also confirm that you will not accept payments in connection with the following businesses or business activities: (1) any illegal activity or goods... (22) sales of firearms, firearm parts or other devices designed to cause physical injury... (24) drug paraphernalia... (25) occult materials [sic] (35) fulfillment houses and (36) network member payment processing service providers.

(25), without explanation, is somehow generically evil?

Question: What on earth are "fulfillment houses"? Because, Mummy, now I want one!

[1] Attila the hun was regarded in past centuries as an ancestral ruler of the *Hungarians*, but this is now considered to be inaccurate. 1. It is believed that the origin of the name *Hungary* does not come from the central Asian *hunnomadic* invaders, but rather from Magyar tribes that were part of a Bulgar alliance called *on-ogur*, which in Bulgar Turkic meant (the) ten arrows: They entered what is now Hungary in the 7th century CE. 2. The *house of Árpád*, established as rulers of the region somewhere between the 7th and 9th centuries of the common era was heavily christianized. Seven members of the dynasty were canonized or beatified by the roman catholic church; therefore, since the 13th century the dynasty has often been referred to as the "kindred of the holy kings."
[2]   https://www2.health.vic.gov.au/public-health/infectious-diseases/disease-information-advice/plague
[3] Joined Britain as a *united kingdom* during the *union of crowns*, 1603, under james 6th, officially in 1706: The parliamentary *union of Scotland* act.

TIMELESSNESS

AN INTERVIEW WITH LINDA BRINCKMAN, HOBART, TASMANIA

Linda: But we're born, we live, we die, yes?
Lore: That's a simplistic and objectified way of understanding life, yes. But everything is complex, and life is not that simple because nothing comes from nothing, so there can't be nothing.
Linda: What?
Lore: My son got into trouble when he was just a kid, for disagreeing with his math teacher when she said zero means nothing...
Linda: Explain?
Lore: (chuckling) Genealogists and geologists are not dissimilar, but we get troubled by modern terminology, like Australia and France. There're no such places, and Australian and French... there's no such people.
Linda: *Genesis | the Future* is written from an age that seems about a thousand years from now. Do you believe the events prophesied in the beginning will happen?
Lore: They already are. And it's a few more millennia than that.
Linda: But you made the story up, yes?
Lore: I'd like to think I did. I'd like to think I was a respectable storyteller. I'm pulling on multiple sources though, and a lifetime of reading everything from Yeats and Poe to the biblical *old testament*;

from the *Edda* and the *Book of Kells* to creation stories from many indigenous cultures. No, I'm filling in the blanks to hopefully make it worth a read.

Linda: When did you get the idea for this work?

Lore: I realize it's always been there. I grew up under the threat of a nuclear winter, with countries like England bombing the life out of Maralinga and European nations perpetuating genocide around the world, *Agent Orange* decimating forests in ways that seem unprecedented, to Chernobyl and Fukushima, to the Murray/Darling decimation. The slave trade's still very real, and people have forgotten about Bikini Island and acid rain.

SUMMONING SIGHT

But a ritual, or ceremony... or call it whatever you want... that a few of us worked back in 1990 was the big trigger. In a waking vision experience I thought I was in some ancient Mesopotamian desert and I met a person. They talked to me a while. I don't remember about what. They eventually said, *you gotta go back.* I said, confused, *what*? They said, *you're in the future, you gotta go back.* I came out of that vision shocked.

Linda: So, you think there's hope for the future in the face of climate change and the mess we're making, as a species?

Lore: We need to grow up. Eventually we'll have no choice. I despise the fear mongering, and apocalypse hearsay that pervades the news right now. Memes keep saying "we" when media tell of the necessity to clean up garbage. But that's a god-consciousness delusion. Earth's more powerful. How do you figure all that affects children? Not necessarily the children of peaceful locations; those hooking in, *Matrix*-like, to social media, that is. I'm referring to kids like those in Yemen, just trying to find shelter, just wanting someone to tell them a cool story. We need to teach our kids, not scare them as much as is happening. I sometimes think it's worse than bashing them with a brick.

Linda: The story doesn't end?

Lore: Stories don't end. Not ever. Not really. They just take a breath.

Kind of like that movie *Fallen* with Denzel Washington, about an *angel* called *azazel*—and *angel* just means messenger, by the way, forget the fluffy-winged or fallen variety, that's just for kids, like *santa* and *jesus*—where the entity passes from person to person, with the Rolling Stones song *Time is on My Side* as the theme.
Linda: So, time doesn't exist?
Lore: Can you tell me when we are? If you remove the construct of dates, I mean? Couldn't this be a few thousand years after Sabé finds the people in the desert? I mean, I don't remember the book now (I've read from before the internet), but I think it might have been The *Head of God* where the author writes about the stories of people ascending clouds into the sky, and about a certain bush that burned like an oil well, or like, in *ezekiel* where a biblical fiery, airborne chariot gets described, by the author's colleague at NASA, as a lunar landing module with more wheels.
Linda: You read tarot. You predict the future. If time doesn't exist how can that happen?
Lore: Just think for a bit about the idea of the hypothetical *big bang*—despite the realization that nothing does not exist—and you were there, right? You're the particle, energetic outcome, that we understand as now, of the hurtle through space of all that light and all that matter. Only light happened instantly. Now light is both particle and wave, so it can be starlight from a distant galaxy that might not have existed for several billion years as we know years to be, but it's still here. So are the events that happen to you. As soon as they've happened, they cease to exist anymore. They're just a memory. They leave a ghost, of sorts. Something we can gauge or reference if a similar thing happens to us or anything we recognize. That's why indigenous people around the world keep such amazing records of things.

But many of us haven't. Or we don't think we have. But then, which *we* are we talking about? Just the few literate bits of humanity. We are only taught, currently, by book-learned teachers.
Linda: I'm in the story, aren't I? Are you the person named Ghost?

Lore: Everyone can recognize themselves in a real story or, I guess, can
empathize.
Linda: What's an unreal story?
Lore: Sad, isn't it? Unreal stories are those that don't have roots in the world. That's what I focus on in these workshops. Ripping the concrete from the flesh of stories that don't move us, and that harm us and others by forcing unacceptably caged stereotypes into consciousness. I work at that with all my stories. A friend once said, of the massive fossil fuel revolution, that we're homeopathically releasing once-living organisms into earth's external atmosphere. Forests and critter-cousins from oh, 650 million years ago. Age of the dinosaurs and all that. Well before a few ice ages which were estimated at about 2 million years ago, and that lasted till about 11, 000 years ago. That's *time* for you. Curiosity and speculation. We're actually not quite out of the last one, hence the concept, in the book, of the southern pole melting.

Not at all far-fetched. According to the theory of super continents Gondwana, that included both so-called *Australia* and so-called *India*, also included the continent of the *Antarctic*.
Linda So, stories are a way of making sense of the world?

Lore: Stories *are* the world.

...

DESCENDING THE BONE SCAFFOLD

HEALING CULTURAL TRAUMA

So long as a conquered people speaks another language than their conquerors, the best part of them remains free.

—Charles De Gaulle

DIGGING *CELT* FROM A DESECRATED TREE

A 'passage grave' is actuality an initiatory womb within earth

We have been given garbled, sacrificially righteous *'us and them'* stories. Of firstly the colonizers of vast, worldwide indigenous landscapes, their descendants and (of seemingly lesser importance in the matter of this topic) human people, that have been slaughtered, scattered and disenfranchised as a consequence. What is the logic behind this arrogance? Of the perpetrator? The thoughtlessness of those who, in the wake of military and religious oppression, systematically steal and settle territories that, for countless generations, have been hunting grounds; contained the lore and *are* the lifeblood and memory; of people.

None of the above includes our relatives of forest, fur, fin, stone and soil. Also decimated.

THOUGHTLESSNESS

It is thoughtlessness that needs interrogating, because hidden in plain sight is our real history. Not taught by parents and grandparent, not by schools, and never by governments, politicians or clergy. Those colluding with injustice, through intent &/or apathy.

Thoughtlessness is passed up the splintered bone and razor-wire scaffolding, even made from their own mothers' ashes. From the deep crevasses and burial caves an ancestral dead whose outraged keening rides winds and storms, any of countless and continuous weather-related *deadlies* moving over the whole earth, their howls rarely—if ever—recognized as a language, let alone heard. Let alone listened to. Let alone understood. Let alone claimed.

During the 1960s, when Australia enacted war on the landscape and the people of Vietnam, in the name of a kingdom and a republic, I woke up from some weird hypnotic sleep. I began to seriously question everything claimed as historically, socially and morally acceptable. Two friends, both in their teens, were killed in that war. The stereotyping of non-Anglo cultures was finally becoming an uprising outrage, as was the realization of the suppression of women.

CHIEFTAIN (*WOSALJAXTO*)

Claiming *Celticness* was, in retrospect something to which I could identify as a young person, but generally, and in retrospect, without the wisdom-minutiae of ancestor training. Rather it was born of a desire to belong to a culture that was plausible—more authentic, and more richly woven into an animist and nature-related tapestry than that of a rapacious English monarchy, adorned with the diamonds, rubies and pearls stolen from the lands of Africa and India, and under whose jurisdiction, and that of her forbears, culture after culture has
been plundered and decimated.

How could we have known? We had been cuckolded into a false self-identity and a network of lies. Forty years ago, there was little to no information on historic Celts. Nothing on king Leopold. No uncensored history. Bylines of *Britannia Rules the Waves* propaganda in Australian newspapers. What I read, about us, was repetitious and, in the *lingua-franca* of the current era, fake news: *The Celts began around the Austrian alps, as the* beaker peoples, *and they spread out across Europe, through Spain, and came to live on the islands of Britain and Ireland.*

Were the facts that simple and that stupid? It's what we were told. No. Not even that. In the school system of the decades following the dirty bombs, our ancient history consisted of Greece and Rome—their empires, their civility, their philosophers, their mathematics (stolen from Arab scholars) and their men (exclusively) of renown; the splendor they brought to the conquered. A little about cyrus of Persia, alfred, called *the great,* genghis khan and chris columbus. Of Hypatia, or any other woman, with the exception of henry 8th's daughter, elizabeth, her religion and her virginity, and her murder of her sister, there was nothing.

TERRA NULLIUS

Modern history? England's approved sailors, anchoring their boats in an alien cove, establishing a fledgling British colony and declaring *terra nullius*. More ships deporting the orphaned and the suffering from London, Dublin, Glasgow and Liverpool and calling them criminal for the sake of expediency. Establishing a slave class to work the stolen lands. The imposition of wheat, sheep and coalmines.

This immigrant migration was, and became, the subject and liege of some enforced *united kingdom*, a mainly-christian, privileged moneyed over-class, some with convict grandparents who, hey! *Gained their freedom and were granted parcels of land and hey!* are also the soldiers who killed their quota of natives that refused to wear aprons or track their own cousins to save their own children (a retrospectively pointless desperation), the Anglo/European aristocracy denying wrongdoing by saying *but they're godless,* from a behind-the-hand snigger of naughtiness. Nothing was *ever* taught to us of the slaughter, rape, stealing or indentured enslavement of First Nation people. Those files were locked away in the archives in Canberra, and the *white Australia policy* was written into law.

This is true the world over, I now know. Tell them nothing but what we want them to hear, and they will be obedient and pliant. Joyful and proud even. They will buy white goods and coca-cola and believe
the delusion of the *great Australian dream* of owning property and, later, from the 1990s during the *john howard* administration, that this continent has a genuine cultural identity. Even though that identity has never been extrapolated beyond bilious talk of a *fair go, fair dinkum, mateship, cricket, acubra hats and crocs* and *What beer do you drink?*

    CELTICNESS

In the 1980s an ideal of *Celticness*, while inclusive of all other cultural identities, was personally entrenched. As a young mother, then, I was still under-educated, aware of Roman invasions of the British islands, of the woman called, incorrectly, Boadicea [1] and her revolt against the *inntrenger*, of the war against Ireland, the protestant revolutions in England, and that Australia was a misnomer, its history a stylized propaganda. I think I was still caught up in the romance of *celticness* whilst, by now, an *amatore* (for the love of it, not a beginner with no experience, known as an amateur) hunter and gatherer of lore and history, as intent a student as could possibly be... considering that I lived in the neopagan-ness of the countryside of the state called *victoria*, with three kids, near-poverty and a genuinely limited inter-library system. No wikipedia in 1983.

I knew that I was cast out. Sold, a rejected human animal, for a goodly sum in a scam that is now understood to be child trafficking. I knew that the woman who bore me was English. The woman who owned me had told me so, in 1972. She begged me not follow up on the information (that she secreted away again, no sooner had she spoken) while she was alive. She wept in embarrassment that I had been lied to, for an entire life, in the same breath that she threatened me to keep schtum. I had agreed. Quizzical. She lived until 2001.

Everything changed in 1984 when two things happened: Callum, the fifteen year old son of Irish/Celtic scholar friends, wrote the *year nine* history exam, taking the part of the British in the war between the indigenous tribes and Rome. He had been failed. Completely. His history teacher had confidentially told him that everything he had written was well-documented, but that the knowledge was not sanctioned. Was not in the curriculum. She was sorry.

SORRY

Family and friends lived at the base of *mount Kooroocheang*, named for the ibis that still came to the area every year after winter. Local legend had it that the aboriginal tribe, named for the mountain and the birds, came from wherever they had been for the other times of year, to join local tribes, for corroboree, on the flat land on one side of the mountain. There were said to be only a hundred or so of them, and that, one year, they had stopped at the homestead of John Hepburn (the local village and springs outside of Daylesford are named for him) who had claimed the land and built himself a bit of england. One of the people, with enough language of the usurper, had requested food. It is said that Hepburn had his housekeeper make a stew and got her to lace it with strychnine. That he murdered the entire tribe.

It had been difficult enough to learn about Wounded Knee and vivisection. It was impossible, then, to learn about Bussamarai, Calyute, Troganinni, Jandamarra, and Kickerterpoller of tasmania and, of course, the great, mystic and seemingly unkillable Pemulwuy, a Dharug warrior of the Eora people who lived around where the ship named *endeavour* dropped anchor, claiming territory that was and never would be theirs.

BONE AND STONE

Our histories are twisted like the rope that hung around many a rebel throat. Resistance and rising through the years. We've lost good me shed blood and tears. It's time for England a truth to face. They will never defeat the Celtic race. Scots and Irish we are one. Our people, our culture, our Gaelic tongue.
—Maire McNally, *We're Celts* (sometime in the late 1800s)
THE RESPONSIBILITY OF A KNOWLEDGE HOLDER

Fast forward to recent years. When I have become an elder human. When I have learned, to an extent, a realistic history of the treatment, decimation, perpetual ignorance and patronizing of the First Nation people. Here, elsewhere, everywhere. A woman born into a landscape not her own. A generic person, stamped *English* by matrilineal descent, called a *white woman*, like it means something that this pelt is pale. But I also learned of the roman invasions and settlements of now-European indigenous lands.

Those of the islands of the Britons and those that kept coming and coming after Rome. Of the imposition, within three hundred years and through force in the main, of the religion of a tortured and dead god. I did not, in those early nineties know the tribal names of the individual confederacies, or stories beyond Vercingetorix of Gaul, that of Budega or her partner Prasutagus, of that bastard emperor Claudius, the second army to land at what is now Kent, or that Tacitus had kept records that would inform us of what really happened. I had yet to learn of the suspect betrayal, by Cartimandua (or so the propaganda is written—it *would* be a woman, wouldn't it?) of my ancestors, the burning of Londinium or the destruction of Mona (the isle of druids) by the emperor's rottweiler, *paulus suetonius*.

But I knew enough. I also acquired a rather substantial library of notes and books pertaining to the *crusades*, and the papal/Norman takeover of the now-Saxon, Danish and Viking settlements and fortresses. That England had become France, and that France built all the castles. All the cathedrals. Of the inquisition, the grand scale impoverishment of folk regions, both in the British-*ish* islands and Europe, by the armies of a, by now, all-conquering christendom, the *malleus malleficarum* trials for the crime of a supposed *witchcraft*, and the murder of—mainly—women, estimated to be in the millions, (their homes misappropriated, and doled out to soldiers, snitches and monasteries alike).

The suffocation, more pervasive than any plague, of what might have once been lore, with the exception of confused snippets, often polluted and tainted by monkish interpretation, kept hushed and garbled by the people who once claimed the landscape as mother, and passed down the generations until, thought superstitious gibberish told by an odd and doddering remnant of a once-barbarian and heathen culture. The secret of the red and white toadstool, of Rapunzel's long hair, of *Sleeping Beauty's* seasonal meaning, the real reason the Pied Piper did what he did, of what a fairy isn't. Distilled into imbecilic saccharine, aimed at children, by the time of the *little golden book*.

Then the woman who claimed the inappropriate and untrue title of *mother* died. The Internet manifested, and the australian government uncaged the hitherto iron-barred information act on *the misappropriation of a human being by graft*.

I then learned who—or *what*—I am.

By now you might think this is just about me. I am irrelevant to this story, in the long run, because I will, anywhere from five minutes to forty years from now, be dead and forgotten. But this is likely *your* ancestral lore. Most of you with the blood of Europe in your veins. And if this is not a song of your ancestral tree, and you are of another branch entirely, then it is a gift to you. A voice against bigotry, because a travesty such as that only exists when someone thinks they are better than someone else. And knowledge, and the sharing of ourselves, shuts that up. It becomes realized for what it is: a contrivance from which someone seeks to benefit, from stepping on
the back of someone else.

DESCENDING THE FRACTURED BONE SCAFFOLD

We descend with great care. And the rungs that support us, precariously, are genealogy, archaeology, anthropology and the many threads of our story learned and understood mainly from the threads of our story learned and understood mainly from the cultures of others. Ours buried beneath a rubble so profoundly messy that the first rungs of this scaffold are treacherous indeed. Made of twigs, where once great forests of Oak spread from horizon to horizon. Made of the fossilized bones of Elephants with straight tusks. Of Bears that once roamed across the landscape of our Ancestors, that now adorn the second-named Elizabeth, and her *grenadier guard*, their mothers and grandfathers only a memory. In the Highlands. Amidst the Cairngorms. In Llyn Trawsfynydd. On what remains of the druid isle, now called Anglesey. Of Elk and Reindeer.

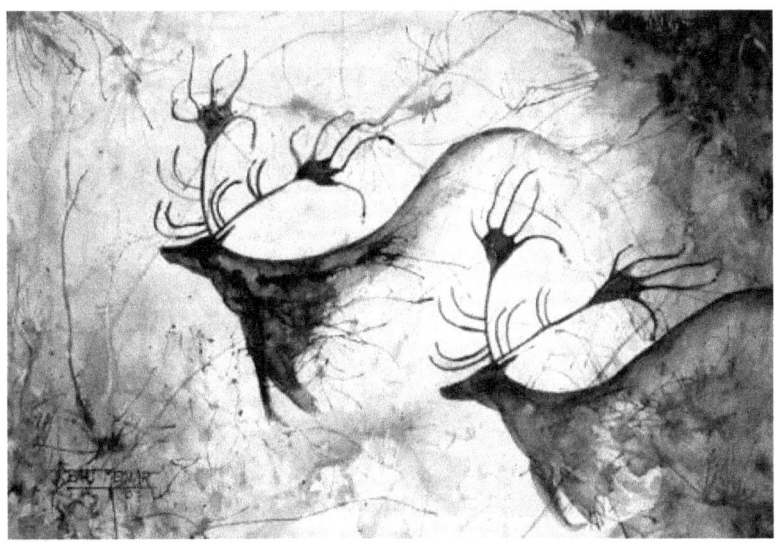

Of the *monarch of the glen* whose carved antlers dug the deep, acoustic song places: chalk ditches 30 meters deep and 30 meters wide, around Stonehenge, around Callanish on Eilean Leòdhais far to sea in what's known as the *Outer Hebrides*, the one surrounding Avebury. The gathering places of Singers and Dreamers and Seers.

A *bailiú sóisialta rialto,* for trade and to arrange *marriages* and allegiances. We so often suffer a profoundly illogical loneliness and homesickness for somewhere and something we cannot, anymore, name. And so, the pejorative *sins of the father* are all our spirits have been allowed to know.

ROME 1, SCOTLAND 0 – NO LONGER ALBANACH CAN WE BE

The reality is altogether another story, and Calgacus' accusations, screamed over the heads of an amassed roman army on the day of the massacre of ten thousand people on the field of *Mons Graupius* 1934 or so years gone by of: *You give us a wasteland and call it peace* rings as loudly today as the words of the *Uluru Statement from the Heart*.

This scaffold is built on the bones of slaughtered ancestors whose songs have become louder and fiercer the older I get. They are an albatross around the neck that I carry because I broke the spell. Because a grandfather, of many generations, also fought. And he let himself become known to me.

What of those raped by alien invaders? This story is from before them. These are your bloodline ancestors also. This is our collective lore.

STORY AND LORE FROM THE DEEP

This scaffold, no matter how fragile, is here to support us as we chisel the filth of abandonment from the Bones of, not only our elders, but those of our children now and those yet to be born. In the era of what science predicts as "the sixth mass extinction", carrying one's deeper story—not of self, but of our connection and communication with an ancientness that I propose links us, web-like, with all other peoples and beings of earth—is a gift.

...

ON BEING ANONYMOUS AND LOST

(Dedicated to the survivors of war, and the children who wait)

As we, in the southern hemisphere, travel around the sun, towards *samhain*, we march, with bruised and blistered feet to the drums of *anzac day*, that glorifies the most tragic of untaught histories. A seemingly endless progression of forgotten tragedies, with only the slouch hat, seeming so heroic, being blathered about when it was people, and forests and species of every cousin imaginable that never understood.

ANONYMOUS AND LOST

And each person fights a little or a lot, to stay alive, and have a life worth living, despite everything. So, when we are anonymous and lost, we all tend to invent ourselves. When we do not have a mirror or an ancient story to hear and know to be true. When we make trouble, when we don't do what society demands, when we don't behave in an appropriate way, we're going to be subject to criticism. Be warned. You and I might be thought of as ornery, or pig-headed or even somewhat arrogant. A fool. A freak or a piece of work. But what about when that's an insult because it is simply untrue, and others choose to see the world through a different kind of sight?

One way of living with being anonymous and lost happens because there is no one to offer us true stories. One way is to become sullen. Resentful. Or work like crazy to fit in. I understand that. Loneliness is the way of the edge-dweller. But I must say that even though this is a track through the forest that myth suggests drove *merlin* mad, it is not the path only trodden deep by Deer, but Wolves in hunt of Deer.

Because there comes a time when the pretense is like an old Seal skin hanging on the back of the kitchen door that used to belong to a *selkie* (who abandoned it long ago). It smells of rot. And that's what'll happen to the person in this one thing.

> *Stories instantaneously bypass the ego. The ego cannot absorb the entire pith of story. The story as a form of entertainment. While the ego is kept happy, thinking it is being entertained, the soul and the spirit are listening deeply. Images in stories is medicine—similar medicine to listening to the ocean or gazing at sunrises. No direct interaction has occurred—the ocean did not jump into your body and fill you. But there is something about seeing, hearing, and smelling the ocean that has bypassed the ego, and straightened out many things that were in disarray within the psyche.*
>
> —Dr. Clarissa Pinkola Estes

While I'm curious regarding her use of the word "ego" in this way, I agree with the sentiment so...The other thing is to learn. Now, that can be a labyrinthine, maze-like endeavor, because not all information that passes itself off as knowledge, is knowledge. Much of it has been copied from the notes of another student. Right when the exam was on. And there's me thinking that person must have the right answers because I didn't understand that the study was open to questioning.

Despite the deceptions and the acceptances along the way, I became a gatherer. And I know many, many gatherers. Some are Scholars and Teachers, certainly, but the best amongst them are the Storytellers, Questioners and Hunters. Modern interpreters of myth and spirituality. The challenger of what spirituality even means.

The center of the maze is what happens if we get there. It's the realization that hidden within everything we have learned just might be a something. But the center of this maze is an unborn child. A puppy still unlicked within a caul. An egg nestled deep within lore...

And, so, here it is then. No way to deal with this world as a person-critter.

People have been too often, and untruthfully, too much at the center. Not the myth and who we are with that. Myth is a story without an author. It's been passed through the generations like some legendary vine. And myth is also the soil in which the vine gains strength. From which all of us, who walk that edge and beg that Cloud to Rain on this Desert of shallow verbiage, unfurls from seed to stem to root to bud to leaf to Fruit.

I was no one. I was lost. I was a cinderblock tenement. An orphanage of abandonment. You know it, or you wouldn't still be reading. There are ropes around our wildness. Some are rough and cruel, yes, but some are silky and seemingly languid, and they are as intentional as chain.

Mother Death walks with us from the day we are precariously born. Don't fear her, because she is the mycelium and the humus, and the future destiny of everything. Everything and everyone, no matter the species or edifice. You'll doubtless still be here when Uluru is as small as a grain of sand.

...

BONE WOMAN

LA LOBA – THE BONE WOMAN

In the long ago when the world made sense and humans didn't do so much talking, wolves ran free across the world. Then the new people manifested from some hidden old greed-land, that the Badger folk forgot to close the door to, and they decimated the people of the old ways, killing their stories which were also their souls. Killing off the Wolves if the Wolves were their totems. Scared of everything.

There are hides and hollows and hedges in the world where the Otter people and the Raven people still live, keeping the stories of the long ago alive for those willing to listen.

The story of La Loba is that of an old Woman living hidden in plain sight in places that everyone knows that most people don't know. Clarissa Pinkola Estés says, "She's been seen travelling south in a burned-out car with the back window shot out... or riding shotgun with truckers" [1].

When she's not getting up to mischief with other Animal People La Loba gathers the bones of the long dead wolves that lie white under moonlight, scattered across the ancient land, until she has a complete skeleton. Then throughout the depths of night she works her magic, finally giving her breath. Come dawn the wolf is enchanted into life, yips with laughter, licks her face, pauses for mere seconds before running, wild and delighted, toward the tree-line.

When I first learned this story, I thought it just another folk tale because I didn't understand. Now I do. She has been in a desert that sooner or later we all travel. A seemingly barren place that, in truth, is not. Finding sustenance there can only happen with familiarity and through the teachings of the old people who know these stories.

La Loba is in every woman, as is the wolf, as is the free woman she becomes.

The many mythic people in this story are to remind us that we are all still in the long ago. That the people in mythworld are very real and that we are being fooled by Creatures not always like us. Not always with our stories or our best interests at heart. That we have as much right to be here as they do. That they should not fear us just because they do not recognize the way of us.

We must protect La Loba wherever in the world she turns up. Offer her a cup a coffee and a place beside the fire. A bed for the night in exchange for what's in that pouch hanging off her belt or what she's got clutched tight in that fist.

Or in her remembering.

Or maybe just because of the relief we feel when she comes to our door in the first place.

TO REMEMBER

I have unlocked the stories in our bones. Memories of ancient primordial uplands in which I hunted, making love beside a vast still lake.

Remembering a dead mother's skin still lies there, remembering running silently between towering Spruce trees in the Snow, following the Reindeer along deep ancestral tracks. Father born on the pelts before the fire pit in a house made of earth, his mother and aunties chanting birthing spells low in their throats, and the small wide eyed children of the Horse keeping vigil until the heavily tattooed old woman bites the cord. His child is me. A thousand generations ago you and I were there. Nothing has gone.

Life has changed and many have suffered an unbearable isolation because no one has reminded us of who else we are other than beyond the current skins we wear.

Eldritch, a human being who is also a Walking Man of long-lived witchery, explained the Celtic word *hiraeth* to me as homesickness, a longing, deep and inexplicable because we don't know what home is. The suffering this causes. Dispossession is in our marrow and that fear, beneath the surface we present to the world, of lovelessness and plastic and asphalt, crowding us into a corner from which we cannot escape.

Initiation is a mapped and charted experience that many people do not understand or recognize when the experience is not on their terms. You will be woken up. When wolf mother takes us in her jaws and pulls us into the myth, we must realize we are helpless. Myth is not fallacy. Myth is as real as the skin that keeps our rawness clothed. Joseph Campbell, in *Hero with a Thousand Faces*, explains initiation as firstly a *threshold*. We die to who we have been. And yes, always tragically. We cross into the *liminal world* and become lost. This could last a lifetime if we lack the necessary insight to realize what is happening. We need to be on the lookout then, as we travel the days and nights of desolation and confusion, for the signs of the *return*. We must keep our ears pricked and our tails bushy. There must be a *return*. Someone to know us. To be met and the purpose of this new life be revealed.

INITIATION—THE GAME CHANGER

When we consciously recognize the place in which we currently live as the *liminal world* of not-life we may very well be ready to *return*. We will know. We will meet the *gatekeeper*. This could be someone already there or someone new. They will complement the true us.

This is not like any other compliment. The person is recognized for the depth of them and how far they have climbed from that pit.

Words will liberate the *dark night of the soul*. The gatekeeper speaks to you in words of the lore of this new life. Do we have the guts to walk through? To accept the change with only courage? To leave that lost place, savage forest, mist of futility, cave of self-doubt and take the challenge of being raw, temporarily blind and furless?

No one can hold us should we choose to make this choice, to wear the next mask and to clothe ourselves in this new garment of self. We don't have to cleave to the identity that we thought defined us. Life is art. Life wants experience through who we are and what we do. Wants the lone wolf to run with the pack.

The most recent initiation life threw at me took nine years to learn from, and I didn't know until I reached the other side.

...

[1] *Women Who Run with the Wolves*, Random House, 1992

THE GUILT DELUSION

Excerpt from *Witch | For Those Who are*

MULENGRO

Mulengro is a disease passed from one person to another using seven dysfunctional manipulations:
envy
greed
guilt
deceit
denial
expectation
assumption

When someone attempts to entice, control, coerce or otherwise warp seeming-facts to suit an agenda they will use one or more of these techniques. The only way to prevent despair from overwhelming our well-being is to cease mulengro in our lives. I've done it; several students have done it; most friends have stopped it.

The outcome to being infected by mulengro is *always*—
resentment,
rejection,
blame and
despair

And mulengro *is* infectious. Mulengro is like the *Karpman Drama Triangle*: I read an article about a couple living together. I'll call them *Gabe* and *Kelly* to ensure gender neutrality because this happens in every partnership at least once.

Kelly is at home and Gabe phones from the office, explaining there is an after-work function they are required to attend, and it could go until late.

Kelly asks, *so Gabe, will you be home for dinner?*
I doubt it, says Gabe, *so don't bother cooking for me unless you want to. I can always microwave it later.*
Okay, says Kelly.

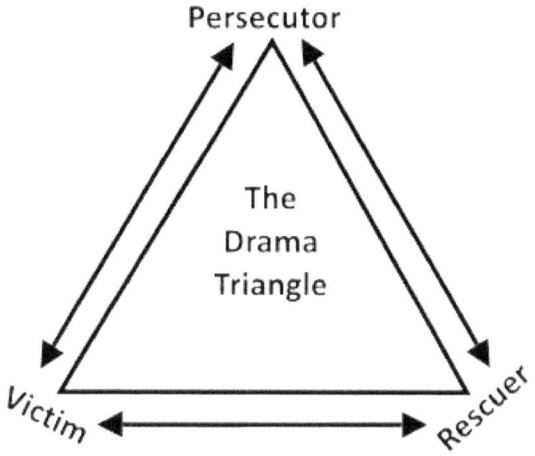

From Transactional Analysis
by Steve Karpman

Oh-oh.

The problem begins when Kelly thinks to make dinner for two anyway, just in case Gabe comes home unexpectedly and is hungry. Partners do that for each other, right? They love each other.

But Gabe does not come home and does not call.

Kelly, alone, does not get on with the evening and read a book. The thought is there, but thoughts also stray to the time, and how late Gabe is. And has there been an accident? Or is Gabe having an affair? Or—

Finally, exhausted, Kelly goes to bed, but cannot sleep because Gabe's absence is now a monster.

At 3 a.m. Gabe comes home drunk, closes the door quietly, removes their shoes and creeps upstairs to the bedroom. Kelly switches on the light:

Where were you? Why didn't you call me? I made us dinner anyway but then it just dried out and was ruined so I threw it away. Why are you so late? What have you been doing? I've been awfully worried. I didn't know whether to call the hospitals or your mother or what! I've been terrified you were mugged or dead.

I've got to pee, Gabe slurs, swaying towards the bathroom.

You're drunk. You've been partying and you're fucking drunk! Kelly bursts into tears.

Gabe returns to the bedroom, undresses, gets into bed and is snoring in seconds.

What just happened? A happy couple is now on the slippery slide to an eventual end. Both are party to the drama triangle, also to every aspect of mulengro. At one stage Kelly enacts all three characters of the triangle whilst both display assumption, expectation denial and envy. Gabe's silence is deceit. It is also denial and greed as surely as it is *gaslighting* and *muting*.

GASLIGHTING

Named for a 1944 film called *Gas Light*. The term refers to a psychological abuse and is used to describe an attempt to destroy another's perception of reality, very often by sociopaths or narcissists, but there are multiple shades of that.

Very often an individual will lie to another, thinking to save them from the hurt of knowing, for example, that they had sex outside the relationship, and both do not want to admit it out of guilt, or wants to keep the external relationship as well as remain in the current partnership. The problem arises when one person's body (gut) gets the jitters. Adrenalin. Bodies read more than intellects and when one knows a partner as well as an intimate partner, or a parent/child relationship, bodies do the talking. Small things. A phone call not returned. A scent one cannot identify. Over time unknown patterns arise and the person being *gaslit* can become extremely ill. Anxiety. Fear. Confusion. If they ask the partner if something is going on that they should know about, and the partner says no. The relationship is, again, doomed. At the extreme, the victim of gaslighting suicides.

MUTING

When you have something important to discuss with a sibling, partner, offspring, parent, boss, misbehaving or inappropriate work colleague and they suggest you stop bitching, moaning, whining, complaining, they are muting you. They say, *I don't want to discuss the matter*, or *you're talking out of turn*, or *I don't want to hear this again*. Or, *you want to keep your job?* Do you do it?

It's aggression. It's avoidance. The person raising the topic is effectively shut down. It can be threatening. You run the risk of being cast out, unloved, unemployed, disbelieved. How do we function as a society?

The need to tell the facts. To also admit when we're wrong. To not inflict these psychological violations onto people we love or admire when we would not inflict them on a total stranger.

Because all the above are dishonesties. They seek to avoid personal responsibility. Accountability.

AUTHORITY

What connotations. The word *authority* has come to represent a pinnacle – the epitome of a powerful person. The word *authority* is quite different, in truth, to a *master* (such as a master carpenter, a master of the sword, a master chef) because a person who has mastered a skill is a practitioner whereas, in many instances, an authority is someone with an opinion who confers with other people with opinions and who, therefore, could be considered educated in opinions. Of *course,* I'm generalizing but it is worth your consideration as quite often those who brand themselves as authorities do not condone having that authority questioned and *that* is, and has been, despotism or tyranny or psychopathy.

Whether the presumed authority is a parent, the president of a company or country, an educator, a five-star general, or a pope, it is the responsibility of an authentic person or society to consider the individual, or the institution, open to fallibility.

I sat enthroned on the dunny of a friend's house, when I was younger, in the Australian state known as *victoria,* pondering the back of the door. The image, on a poster there, depicted a skeleton in a bathtub, in the bathroom of a hotel that is discovered in the far distant future by a team of archaeologists. They document the sarcophagus (the bathtub), the roll of paper used to send messages to the gods via an aqueduct (toilet paper and flush-toilet), mirror used for divination, various holy objects (like razor, toothbrush etc.) arranged on an altar, the obvious sacredness of water (realized, of course, from the profusion of taps), the quirky plastic crown worn by the king or priest of this temple (the shower-cap). On and on went the description. I understood that no one could fully know the past from the standpoint of the present and that all such sciences employ guesswork.

When I see a documentary on ancient people depicting them bent-over, ugly, hairy primates I tend to cringe, as nothing in life is ungainly in its natural habitat so why depict humanity, alone, as having been so? And *primitive* is merely deemed as derogatory in comparison to us now. To take upon oneself the responsibility of informed questioning ensures that *authority* does not take upon itself the presumption it is better-than another, person, system, lore or knowledge just because it may not understand. It allows for possibilities, it allows for alternatives, it allows for error and it ensures that its own authority remains accountable.

THE JESUS MYTH

Pope Leo X, who reigned in the years 1513 to 1521, said: "*It has served us well, this myth of Christ.*" By this he meant that over the centuries, the vatican managed to acquire enormous wealth and power in the name of an era-characterization it called *jesus christ*. In the twentieth century, the man most responsible for making the Vatican a financial powerhouse was its investment manager, bernardino nogara. Speaking of him, a man named *cardinal spellman*, of New York, once said, "*Next to Jesus Christ, the best thing that ever happened to the catholic church is Bernardino Nogara.*" Anticipating that Europe was heading for war, *nogara* invested heavily in armaments factories, buying several of them outright. This allowed the papistry to reap huge profits when *mussolini* invaded Abyssinia in 1935 and in the second world war later.

RELIGIOUS FUNDAMENTALISM, DOGMA, BIGOTRY

It's driven into children, in war-torn countries, brainwashing them into hating one another without them knowing exactly why. It is the arrogant racist who believes in an imperialist, white supremacy that presumes anything can be bought. It is in the neo-*nazi* and the *ku klux klan*. Fundamentalism is in the office worker next to you who feels her faith is superior to yours and that you will be damned for your viewpoint and your sexual activity and she, to a place thought of as paradise. Fundamentalism is the reason people mail anthrax to abortion clinics because they don't believe a woman should have a right to choose what happens to her flesh-and-blood body.

Fundamentalism is the man who bullies, beats or represses his partner because he believes women are inferior – the source of all wickedness because of some *middle eastern* myth from life only knows how long ago—and passes on seeds of tyranny to his children. Fundamentalism is the people who mock same-sex love; people who shun unwed mothers, the poor, and those infected with HIV-AIDS calling such a terrible illness *"the wrath of god"*. It is people who smile politely to those of another race in public but who condemn them, in private, purely because of the color of their skin or the difference of *their* religion. Religious fundamentalism; religious laws, rules, arrogance, moral condemnations. A sure way of controlling people, don't you agree? Divide and rule?

Divide et impera, the practice has been used socially, politically and militarily since documentation began. Philip II of Macedon (circa 365 BCE) is the first person quoted as utilizing the tactic. *Divide us to conquer us*. Diminish us. Instill doubt, envy, threat, fear. It is happening as I write, in politics. In the year that I write this politics wages a chess game of brinkmanship in league with big business and media. Do we buy into it? The challenge is to *not* allow it to. The challenge is to be very alert but to *not* become angry. They have us when that happens. Should we declare organic food our weapon, or peddle-power, or cloth bags instead of plastic, recycling over the next iPhone, if we should meet in an age of text-isolation, use pencils to remember how to write, gather in large numbers to protest the cruelty of factory farming and the imprisoning of refugees in offshore detention, if we could stand together so that education returns to being education instead of big business, not eat their garbage. Well, I'm with you on that.

The same applies, I am stunned to be informed, that in the post twentieth century *'west'*, spiritual practices known as *paganism*, *shamanism*, *druidry*, *wicca* and some groups that even call themselves *witches*, charge money to teach. To hold retreats. They sell products that we used to always make ourselves. The challenge of this essay alone is for us to learn. For us to hold our freedom and not be undermined because we see what is being done. To learn and keep learning. Then, to unlearn, when necessary, in order to deepen.

To thunder into the future as creatures of Art. A future where wonder is revered, and Wildness, and the beauty that is Life is honored, where such terms as *man conquers... in the battle to control...* and *in the war against...* are no longer used to discuss natural phenomenon like Mountains, Space, Death. Actually, why use this terminology for anything?

RELIGIONS

Religions. What is valid about them? Whom do they serve? Religions demand worship. Rules to die for. They demand divisions and employ dualisms like good and evil, us and them, sacred or profane. Always divisive. Religions and the words *worship, faith, belief* all to go together. Inherent within these words is possibility of doubt. When we can gather for feasting and mutual learning, creating a barn, a community, a cleaner environment, without religion to bind us, we'll have achieved a *grail quest*.

Many denominations and cults demand tithing, and blackmail, to ascertain entry into a presumed afterlife. The conscious smashing of this false idol of what is, beyond the confines of orthodoxy, a vital and energetic animism, is worthy of deep discourse. We, rightfully, need to ask permission of what we are to consume, before any move on landscape is made; before any food sources are killed.

Before any more secret poisons are added to sly and coerced sleep; to apathy.

...

NOTE

The spelling mulengro is a shortening of the form *mulengero*. This shortened form is used quite commonly in some varieties of Romani < mulhengero *mulo* (fog ghost*), mulengero di (all souls day), mulo (dead)* [these terminologies are from the Burgenland Romani dialect]

LANGUAGE OF ANIMACY
Rewilding the Magical Narrative

We *draíocht*-people are edge-dwellers. Often living oddly, through necessity, on the clifftops and in the caves of mythworld. Many have fallen or jumped because they cannot pretend to be what others want them to be. Sometimes because they haven't a language that does not sound like a made-up version their mothers or sisters have heard in a trashy movie. Being a lore holder is a way of living that requires paying attention to earth, to patterns and weather conversations, to communicate, perform ceremony and make art, accurately foretell future events including the weather, in language that defies justification.

The word *shaman*, originating from the *Tungus* nomadic herders of Siberia, means *one who sees in the dark*.

Much terminology needs euthanizing. Much that is demanding and thoughtless. Words that ring of the *abrahamic* religions: sacredness, worship, holy, divine, adore. Evoke, summon, banish. Alien to the language of *crop circle* and bog. Neither is it the language of a seventines stag, the iron muscle when you bite into the dead salmon's flesh, the scent of vernix, the howler winds across the Cairngorms, the reek of Goat in musk or the shock of a ribbon-fleshed, Barnacle-encrusted once-woman's body caught on the line instead of brother mackerel.

A LEVEL OF INSIGHT

When, in a story, I wrote the word *firn* to describe the fluff—the pith—in the spine of a goose feather that must be scraped away before glue will take hold, affixing it to the shaft of an arrow, for true flight and a clean kill, spellcheck informed me I was mistaken.

In 2007 the *Oxford junior dictionary* rejected the following words, claiming that they do not hold any relevance for today's children, and
replacing them with *attachment, blog, broadband, bullet-point, celebrity, chatroom, cut-and-paste, mp3 player.*

Witchcrafting—that of the wisdom of *draíochta* people—is akin to the workings of *shamanism* or of a *kurdaitcha* but is neither. Not, anyway, for those of us who are neither. Healing the illness of being lost from the landscape of true living takes both talent and a level of insight. Achievable, but never by mimicking the languages of colonizers, thieves of cultural heritage and speakers of misappropriated non-verbal communication and language systems. For a Celto- or Anglo-European, or other northern hemisphere pale-pelted person, living witchery, a level of insight is imperative, as is a hunt for the genuine, because *abrahamic* religions have smothered our language-relationships. To release ourselves is to rewild ourselves. To live authentically.

Witchcraft is also claimed as the title of a ritualized religion called wicca that, trendingly and machiavellianly, continues to divide into splinter groups. Holistically all have a *gardnerian* core, and none can, or need, prove otherwise. While not an intentional defense, all of these practices are recent, and follow a prescription that is neither criticized from within nor accepted beyond irrelevancy by those without. Because of the narrative employed. Most are, however, biased by a binary and anthropocentric perspective that is divisive and promotional of unintended bigotry.

Remaining in a communication dichotomy is imprisoning. Poetry and Rhythm, Chatter, Weather-Talk and Song are the doors to freedom. Our way of communicating with everyone from Horse to Cloud.

However, Naming, whilst treacherous, can also liberate a unique person (no matter a species) from the trap of a noun. And the insidious habit of ownership. *My* mother. *My* father. *My* town, *my* country, *my* religion, *my* thoughts... Can't even own a body when we're dead.

...

BROKEN TONGUE

The Subtle Bigotry of the English Language

Inglan is a bitch, Dere's no escapin it. Inglan is a bitch
Deres no runnin whey fram it
Mi get a lickle jab in a bih otell
An awftah a while, mi woz doin quite well
Dem staat mi aaf as a dish-washah
But w'n mi tek a stack, mi noh tun clack-watchah

—Linton Kwesi Johnson

Certain acquaintances send me private messages explaining that a recently written work needs a good editor. I always respond, asking about the glitch. Happy if they've been disturbed by a spelling error. But that's not what this is about. When I discover, as I invariably do, that what so offends them was intentional when I wrote the words or the story, I don't justify. I don't even reply.

I understand the need for certain stops. Certain punctuation. Even Daughter will pull me up with *Mother!* if I use *ain't* instead of is *not* or *isn't*. But the English language is an absolute mongrel of pompous stealth and misappropriation. So, I'll write *er gar, ya mucky feeblie blarner ruckin stuckler fucker, yer all drookit!* and feel no remorse.

When I was a child, I was forced to attend a gender-segregated kindergarten, and was warned, through the thin line of the headmistress's juiceless lips, that trained attack dogs patrolled just outside the gate and that they would rip me apart if I tried to leave the grounds without permission. I endured elocution lessons, because the sprawling drawl of this young colony was becoming louder. The offensive laziness of the lower classes. And there. Bigotry inherent in language.

Today's new *cool* is allowing your dialect to be popular, *eh by goom lad.*

I have tarot clients from all around the world. Immigrants and refugees, with strong accents that require acute listening to understand. But. And here's the crossroads. I *only* speak one language. I can count in five others, say hello in as many and could also ask for a *cafe con leche* when in Spain. The people who have learned english as a second tongue are amazing. And I am the fool.

BANISH THE BASTARDS

When you write—if you write—banish the bastards who condescend to correct your dialect. Be loud and proud.

We are only now beginning to free ourselves from an archaic academia, steeped in latin, the verbiage of conquerors, rapists and thieves. Bigots. And many studies, like biology, botany and medicine, retain their roots in that language. Dead as a body buried in landfill. The fucking empire is desiccated. The final death-roll of this antediluvian beastie is this adhesion to grammatical correctness.

MY COCK IS BIGGER

The jutting chin of rapacious privilege exposing genitals for us all to admire, effectively saying, *my cock is bigger than your cock.*

Next time you hear that subtle inner voice pigeon-holing another person, by their ability to speak this mongrel tongue, as under-educated or not sufficiently literate, go look in the mirror. I done it, once upon a time. Or should I say *I did*?

You get time, read Robin Wall Kimmerer's work, or watch her chat on YouTube. Robin is a Potawatomi woman, and a scholar, and trying to get her brain around the Anishinaabe language. Realizing the sorrow of a vast forgetting, when she explains *puhpowee*. When I first read her, I was writing a memoir. *Oh, please*! I thought the sender, an adviser on that writing at the time, was hinting. I'd promised, understand, that I could story the language of wildness and freedom now. I was a grown up. Didn't need to denigrate the shadow anymore. So, under seeming-advisement, I rewrote as much as I could, eradicating 'it' as often as possible.

When I contacted her much later, proud and thankful as a puppy that she'd sent me Robin's essay, she'd come back with, *Oh. No, darling. Sorry. I just thought it was a good article.*
'It?'
'GOOD?'

Me? I'm a mongrel, an absolute mongrel, smattered with the pale dermis and blue veins of the Breton, Parisi, Irish and Alban, freckled with Nordic logging activity. Mother's people spoke *lanky*. I love language. Mainly because of etymology. To know the true meaning of the so-called slang word chook is from the old Irish *cheogh,* and that means hen.

You lose your native tongue? Someone's stolen your identity and said you ain't cultured enough.

...

BEING REAL

IN AN AGE OF DUPLICITY

Do we ever really listen to our seemingly random thoughts? If so, can we discern the different *layers* of thought? Do we think about what we say when we say it, or do we find ourselves repeating material in a repertoire? Do we communicate, internally, with someone or something that we know is not self?

HUNTING VALIDITY

What, to you, constitutes authority? Do you have unique thoughts and/or *original* conversations or are they based on pre-learned parameters? Do you question everything that you are told or taught? Do you question yourself on issues, ideals, ideologies, beliefs, ethics, moralities and information upon which you base your judgments or opinions? Do you change when the above is undermined, or do you insist on being seen as consistent? When listening to another person speaking, do you listen without bias?

Answering these questions can change us. Especially if we allow ourselves to answer freely and to enter debate regarding the questions, our answers and what we really feel in the depths of us. Does anyone even care? Does it matter? Does anyone you know care? Are we living in a vacuum?

THE PRACTICE

The practice has nothing to do with talking and everything to do with listening. Listening very deeply. Listening deeply requires that we use more than our ears. Listening requires that we use our hearing in conjunction with our eyes, our sense of atmosphere: our guts.

The practice requests that... First, we initiate no conversations, we only respond to what is said to us, we do not automatically think of what we will say next. The practice asks us to recognize our pre-conditioned biases and that our emotions respond to all conversations without pre-conceived parameters of relationship.

Second, we observe the body language of the person with whom we are engaged in conversation, we remain aware of the spaces between our bodies as this is a strong indicator of the emotional state of the person towards us, we remain aware of our bodily responses to the conversation and learn to trust them – they are a truer receptivity barometer than our intellect when any precarious content enters into the conversation, we never prejudge a person by the glamour they present, rather we remain alert to the equality of all people, no matter how educated in a so-called western modality.

EXAMPLES OF ROLE

The Arguer: debate, keeping the object of debate at the constant foreground of conversation, does not lead to argument unless the participants become emotionally attached to being right. It is no longer, then, a debate but a debacle that will leave both or all parties debilitated.

The Manipulator: emotional manipulation utilizes many criteria: guilt, flattery, conspiracy, destructive criticism, arrogance, vulnerability, constant agreement, denial, comparison – you can tell which is which, by the inflation/deflation ratio.

The Quoter: this person will use 'the big guns' of authority by quoting the works of others as a reference upon which to base their opinions.

The White-Lighter: well, mostly they don't engage, they just tell you what's good for you and talk at you about stuff that makes them feel good about themselves.

The Perennial Parent: is constantly thinking they know what's best for others based in their own experience, socially, spiritually, morally and emotionally. This behavior seeks to impose uniformity onto individuality without recourse to differences. Many politicians and religious leaders do this. As do people with something to gain. As do those who need a mirror to their own psyches.

The Victim: there are two kinds of victim in the world. Those with choices and those without. Those people who have choices can choose to change their current realities, but the Victim will not, preferring to use that behavior to attract sympathy, to control another.

Real victims (of any species or other life-form) have no choices. They are legion, and altering the ways we both communicate, and listen, are two of their chances of escape. They do not have a voice. They are not heard.

What we do, by actively engaging in this experiment, is to break down, or through, conditioning. We alter our emission—our harmonic—and that influences the collective *world-field*.

Enough alteration: overall change to the human harmonic affecting life.

...

RAZOR WIRE BLUES

1.

A booted foot holding down a mighty length of barbed wire below me, lifting the string of danger from above me, and me climbing through, getting snagged anyway, and shredding a wool sweater. I don't remember *who* and I don't remember *why*, I just remember the wire. The fence, the cruelty of it. Thinking about the bastard who invented it.

Now I sit on a bloody-great rock at the side of the land, careful of the barbs of blackberry thorns—not because of them, per se, but because of the spraying. The poison that is coursing through the undergrowth, taking so many people-species with it. Wrecking the next generation, their shells too thin, their brains addled with concrete. A bit like me, I concede.

So—

Who are we in all this? Cattle of milkers, and baby boys headed for the abattoir next week. Reindeer elder, alone, brought here, to this mother-forsaken tourist trap, how? With a memory of Tundra, I can't even consider? What're you doing inside that fence? Are you inside? Or is that a skewed perspective? Sister Mouse becoming Brahminy hawk (seems like death to the onlooker)? Glossy Raven Mother teaching this summer's young the art of thievery? Wedgetail family gliding the thermals, nothing smaller than a Fox safe from the skill?

This here wire is pathetic, though. The stuff of rust and sag, fifty years old or more. Not like the new shit—razor wire—atop the prison yard, the barricade to keep other people, just like us but, somehow not like us, on some delusional side of reality.

Cattle. Interesting word. It's the word for the day.

Herd. Interesting concept. It's the concept for the week.

The intended strategy was to teach stalking. Did you know that I am a hunter? Bow, not gun. I digress. We'd trudged, mud-deep, through long-neglected landscape at the back of Byron Bay, through swamp and weed-savaged undergrowth, still scarred with barbed wire, although to keep in what, or to keep out what, long forgotten. Finally making the secluded open field. On one side tall scrub, on the other a thick *foresty*-type stand of Sheoaks

We stalked cow cousins.

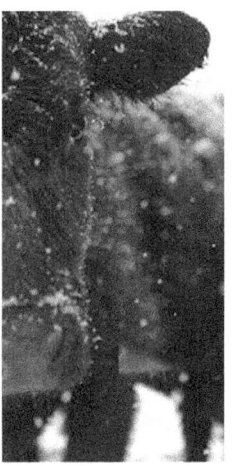

I was so cocky. All the things I thought I knew about being upwind, how to not make a sound. Fifty women and their children. Up ahead. Us in the belly of the unseen. Long-hidden, or so I thought. Ignorant, pale human critter, in cammos, with a compound bow and a quiver of twelve 2118 alloy shafts, fletched in colored plastic, over their shoulder.

Of *course* they knew we were there. I saw their eyes just before they bolted into the deep safety of a green-grey gloom. I remember grinning. Shrugging, defeated. But then *she* came.
That Big Old Bovine Woman. Out from the bush. At a run. Halfway between us and the disappeared crowd. She spread her legs wide. Planted them. Defiant. Stood there, staring us down. Black eyes wide with fear and a knowing. Ready to die. Is that what you decided, Mama? That it would be you, to save the Clan?

I wept a bit, watching her. Comprehending. I don't think I would have that kind of courage. Such respect. We scrambled away. And I am haunted. I don't know what side of the fence is supposed to be the prison.

...

DROWNED

A formal letter of objection to the british/australian government on behalf of non-traditionally acquired children.

To the Department of Births Death and Marriages...

This was once about me but not anymore. Now it is directed to authorities keeping records of other people's progeny. This is about the future.

This yet-to-be-realized future is not on your radar. You don't realize that your name is on the paperwork; you, being a notary and all that seriousness; a bureaucrat—that titling pretense. This letter is about a future that you seem to forget will hold your bones and those of everyone you have ever loved. You need to stop downing that next shot. Now. Lay down that rolled up twenty dollar bill, unline that cocaine and listen to me.

The offspring of this friend, who donated their sperm to a woman in a same-sex relationship, and who requested parental involvement, was born last year, but you don't intend to record the aforementioned friend's name.

In the historical instance this lack of a man's name on the record of a child born to an unwed woman was to protect the identity of the inseminator from ruin. *He* was not to be held accountable or *his* reputation as an upright, god-fearing man would be *tarnished*: Until very recently, most *non-legitimate* children had, due to the circumstance of conception, no absolute way of knowing their biological origin, and had to jump through hoops with possibly dubiously-trusted outcome.

Your legislation is too lazy, or sufficiently remiss, to change a document that records all significant DNA donors, and their relationships to the child.

The angle, here, is on genealogy—heritage and culture—and the accessibility of adequate data for ancestral information and relevance in the so-called future, and although the main focus of this letter is personal—the colonialist and religious arbitration of adoption by non-genetic adults—I am addressing the ineptitude of a currently archaic bureaucracy.

You, keeper of records, are old and feeble-minded.

NEUROLOGY

The break in the mother infant bonding has an enormous impact on brain chemicals and neurotransmitters. Cortisol and adrenaline are raised in trauma, and there are reduced levels of serotonin. These things happen from very early on... 'Where am I' is the constant question.

I sat, once, with a spit tube spit tube. Trying ancestry.com. For the sake of the children that I birthed, and theirs. Out of a profound and organic need to know not only who we are, but *where*.

DNA

So, whose DNA can a female customer use, besides her father's? It could be anyone who shares their Y chromosome — their brother, paternal uncle (father's brother), or even paternal grandfather [4].

But not when you have no knowledge of any of the above because you, and your irresponsible birth certificate system didn't record it, and no one will admit anything. You consider this acceptable. You pompous, misogynous bombast, claiming credibility merely because you are legal.

> *One has not only a legal, but a moral responsibility to obey just laws. Conversely, one has a moral responsibility to disobey unjust laws.*
>
> —Dr Martin Luther King

Legal, also, was the *white australia policy*, was (and is) the slave trade. The burning and torture of women for suspected witchcraft or heresy. Stoning for blasphemy. In many cultures, for loving someone of the same gender. Or the *inferior* caste. Just because it's on paper doesn't make it right. Doesn't ever make it sane.

This donor friend is happy. They will be involved in the upbringing of their child. That is not in any doubt. I am thinking of future generations. I am asking that we take the matter of registration of a human being seriously, for those seeking their heritage and culture in an uncertain future. I am happyish. A name was on a hospital birth record; matrilineal line found. Eventually knowledge of a father and his ancestral line.

Although the truth of this ancestry is real, I could not *legally* claim them as relations, because the law pertaining to the acquisition of children, other than those born to a family lineage, stated that I am not them; that the purchase of the *me*-body meant rules... rules that I, as an adult—and lore holder—had to remain sane and raveled.

The study of genealogy requires documents. Parish records, title deeds, rolls, shipping logs, military service data or census information. Birth certificates, marriage certificates or wills. Everyone has an inherent right to know who they are, where they are from (and, therefore are), and the ways of their heritage and culture. That is currently not the case.

I am a fraud because the law has written me as thus. I am a fraud because sex is—or was—shameful. This document does not go into the politics of marriage, the concept of legitimacy or the processes of breeding. But then, I am not a racehorse or a poodle, both of which require a knowledge of pedigree, am I?

Or am I?

What I do know is that those of us acquired by strangers, often for money, live lives drowning in deceit, swallowing the gall of pretenders and their inability to conceive, or fathoms beneath living air, gasping within oceans of bureaucratic babble.

Write the correct, and sufficient, names into your database. All their names. The names of their progenitors; where they are from.

Grow up.

...

WITCHIN IN THE WILD WOODS

Witchin in the wildwoods, witchcraftin witch tattoos, witchin in the kitchen, cookin mushroom stews, witchin wilding caged things and singin up a storm, witchin be the firebrands that keep the cinders warm.

Witchin takes a beating because no one thinks we're real, but witchin is the hoodoo with the ability to heal. Just remember when you're tired and the world seems so forlorn, we're the nightrise and the moonshine, both the perfume and the thorn. And we know each other always, it's the twitch that's in the grin, it's the daring to do life consciously; accepting, willingly, that we're the juniper in the gin.

Witchery watches spiders while they learn the ways to weave, swap bodies, when we're sleeping, with the owl up in the eaves. We're the howl you dread, from instinct that tells you someone close just died, we can catch you when you're fallin when they find out that you lied. Witchin is a poison to the purist who dares to say you chose the life you live, when you're beaten, and you're busted, and you've got nothin left to give. Witchin hides you from the bigot and the righteous and the tame, witchin takes you to the forest and reminds you of your name.

When witchery's in the kitchen, and is a-cookin mushroom stew, just this once allow the aroma to come on up and summon you, because this life can seem so empty when the magic's been denied, but it's here, within the shadows, in the alleys, in the attic, in the Caves and Walrus hide. You can wear it like the Wolf pelt or the Crane skin or your own skin. Best your own skin... it's the only thing that can never be denied.

That supper's on the table and witchcraft pulls you up a stool; says "stay, and eat, and sit a spell..." Take a chance it isn't poison; that you won't become a toad... or there's the dusty pathway and that long and lonesome road. Say thank you for the invite, for the spoon, the scented steam, cause when you wake up in your own bed you might think it but a dream...

    Except for them muddy Bird tracks across your pillow...

...

TRICKSTER

About now I want to also mention that I have been haunted by what in legend and lore is trickster. Trickster is an entity or spirit, puka or sometimes a god that exists within the myths of almost every culture worldwide. And this beast has sashayed and danced through mythworld, taunting and challenging me for this lifetime. Always riding one man's body or another (only recently recognizable in certain women). For a while. Just like in the movie *Fallen*.

When I did not guess the game, trickster moved from person to person disrupting and obfuscating my liberty. Originally this character of lore presented benevolence. Even at birth. Human beings who desired to control, to own, to direct, even to be protected. Trickster sought an outlet for misbehavior, stealing power, imposing a socially-contrived order, impoverishing.

When I refused to learn of choices, to embody knowledge, to realize when I have acquiesced to the expectations and norms of femaleness, out of laziness or fatigue, trickster discarded the body of the individual whose form they wore. Who was left behind? I don't know. The ones I allowed inside me became daunted and weak. Trickster sucking their strength from them and leaving a wrecked aftermath. They all ended up the same. Fitting into some approved paradigm that didn't work for me or that was just downright ugly in the way of myth: behaviorally.

Trickster exists, also, in the modern psyche. Providing stern lessons. Whether Loki or Crow, Coyote or Puck, Bugs Bunny or Reynard the Fox, Eulenspiegel or Dr. Who, what trickster wants, ultimately, is what everyone wants. Worthy stories. So that living is an experience of granite strength but feather-light malleability. Of excitation and liberty. Duende.

The people I admired or deferred to often initially displayed reciprocity—a seeming empathy—but were, actually, possessed by trickster until I gained all kinds of true strength. Savvy. The capacity to love, or simply experience, without disrespecting hard won core ideals. Without compromise.

From birth until early adult years trickster wore the mythic and illusionary *cloak of authority*. Someone who knew better than I what was good for me. Then, when I turned my back on that archetype—took to anarchy—the tactics changed. Trickster played the sexy card. Became beguiling, seductive. Chose handsome men to wear, to make love with. Trickster persuaded men to persuade me that they loved me.

In the latter encounters I was complicit simply because I was naïve to the real story. Every woman I have ever met wants to be loved. We also have—or I once had anyway—a propensity to stay, even when the relationship was rabid. Even when trickster had abandoned the men weak, broken and bleeding, or violent and controlling, or once again seeking domination because that's all they had left. Trickster wanted nothing less than to meet, face to face, cultural and gendered weakness honestly and deeply abolished. Wanted neediness to be in an intimate partnership, with any traditional affectations, to be the discarded skin of the python discarded, like a strip tease's outer garments, in a mango tree.

To be authentic at this human being business.

To learn the language of animal people.

To break me, see me bleed. Become bone. Allow myself to be clothed in the body of the long-dead wolf and walk freely into tomorrow.

COLOR ME GREY

> *These beautiful trees include an 800-year-old tree that has seen over 50 generations born inside of a hollow in her trunk and a 350-year-old directions tree that has been shaped and resembles a woman.*
> —Djapwurrung Embassy

I moved house just recently. So much to do. Cleaning, decorating; painting. I have so many people to thank, and I will do so later, but this is not about friends. This is about tribe, pack, clan.

THE PORTAL

I wish to hereby reference the *great god bunnings* of the *temple of bunnings*, all her court, her nobles, her wizards, her viziers, her priests, her jugglers and, ultimately, her guides between the world of privilege and the land of myth and magic. Beings of rich hue and versatility dwell within her belly and watch us, mere mortals, with the eyes of—either/or—raptors and chickens. As believable a validation as any other omnipotent deity (who doesn't even have numbered aisles!) created by the imagination of that Darwin bloke's evolved species definition of intelligence.

Do you have the equivalent of *temple bunnings* in the land you call your country? In the lands of Britons, brehons, Bretons? Probably. But not *temple bunnings*. Not always a place of crowds and majesty. Remember her humble beginnings? We have all experienced this, and some of you are still trapped. I wish you well. Bunnings is so profoundly un-Ikea that I weep for joy. This being a tale of magic, witchery and hoodoo however, I must begin at some seeming beginning. As though there ever was such a thing. And if you, or anyone, can presume to actually *say* when events truly begin they are a liar. Or else they have never been to bunnings, so are unaware of the delusion they are feeding to a gullible populace.

> *Shadows on the hills*
> *Sketch the trees and the daffodils*
> *Catch the breeze and the winter chills*
> *In colors on the snowy linen land...*

Bunnings was the brainchild of the bunnings brothers. Hailing originally from *Hackney*, in London, and having arrived on the coast of the west of Australia in 1886, these lads lacked a bit of imagination when they named their business. Still. That's what *david jones* did, and *washington*, and *mcdonalds*. Was *washington* named for a person named *washington*? I could look it up but that could be considered cheating. Wait. I just did.

The bunning boys were given the first-ever contract to destroy enough Jarrah forest (*djarraly*, in Noongar language). To build the first-ever lunatic asylum. Interesting.

SELLOUT

Bunnings did not remain a bunning, however, and is now owned by wesfarmers (you know the ones: $200 million bid for the curragh coal mine in the British/Australian state called, blandly and without initiative, queensland, the acquisition of indigenous ancestral land for demolition and consumption). I think that's supposed to be a secret or something because the current bunnings papistry—the magi and administrators thereof—do not make this deception easily accessible.

Still, people got to have a job, right? (For the purposes of this story, I will temporarily keep schtum regarding 'gotta have a job' dilemma. It'll most likely be an article called after Pink Floyd's *Brick in the Wall*.

I will, at some time, come back to the topic of the stupidity of this doomed ideology but…

The point is the people. The faerie-story Wildlings, and Wisdom-holders, of this tool and trowel empire.

Colors changing hue
Morning fields of amber grain
Weathered faces lined in pain
Are soothed beneath the artist's loving hand…

MR. PAINT, THE WAYSHOWER

Mr. paint walks me through choices. Talks with me as though we are scholars at the university of diversified grey.

We discourse on its varied hues, from fear to fog, peat, arctic winter, Africa, India ink, a goth's black vinyl lipstick or the impossible darkness of a coffin buried six feet below the surface of the landscape, the sight of moles or the leftovers from a crematorium blunder.

From midnight to slate, from dove-wing softness to the harsh reality of almost-black, apartheid, betrayal and despair. How black has become strangled through misrepresentation, like a left hand—sinister—when it is the color I have worn for a lifetime. The black, the color of the pupils in every eye.

It is the reason people take the knee and raise a fist in solidarity with brothers and sisters, children, mothers, elders and those confused, mad, self-medicating or pinned by the neck until dead, because they are proud; a culture that has no word for *time* in the language of ancestors, once ripped from their motherland and transported, like cattle and canaries, across a cruel sea. In solidarity with those unjustly misrepresented. Or massacred in the name of a prophet out of Palestine, a loving *saver-of-something* who didn't even make it to thirty four.

It is the reason we march under the banner of #aboriginallivesmatter because they do, and because history has lied, and lied, and lied, and lied. And continues to do so.

Me? This here pelt is pale where the ink isn't, and is easily seduced by brother sun, but with a heart that is the dungeon of a person who has never walked as ancient lands. Yours, too, perhaps? And only *you* know why I write that. *You* who know me.

We have to. I have to. March, that is. Beside, behind, with. Because the perpetrators of *bland* and *blancmange* didactic iconoclasm continue to spruik and defend a cruelty, an intention, a denied participation in plunder, and the acquiescence, and apathy, of those who take: once in the name of *her majesty queen vikki*, now in the name of lizzie who is destined to die and take her wealth and her titles with her, because who is silly enough to consider a monarch more righteous than you? Or your children? Who are you and what have you lost?

What was taken from you, us: time-worn, commoner crofts seized, for the sheep to live in and with, not people, the lost and confused paleskins sent to this harsh land, allowed to grab and rape and shoot and mutilate, so long as it is only black-bodied people slugged by those plague blankets, destined for absorption into *inntrenger* society by an outbreeding program, an institution called *the church* and residential facilities that some fuckwitted fat boy in a suit, smoking a slave-whipped, virgin-rolled Cuban cigar, and recently arrived from a land far, far away has decided is somehow as righteous as eating the flesh of a long dead tortured fella, a refugee born on the run from genocide (yes, still Palestine), and presenting his *ghost* with brides: little girls in white dresses and veils...

I confided in mr. paint that grey is a color of power. We discussed, in initiatory and druidic tones, the variance between cairn grey, the color of *tòrr* or *cleit* or *creachan*, whether it should reflect the *sìdhean* at midsummer or if we, cautiously, should err on the side of the *bhàn* of *dubh*.

No.

We lighted on *ghlas* or, more appropriately *lèith*, with a shadow, appropriately for a onesome such as me, of the moss that thrives along the base of the *fèith*; a touch of the ruff of sister wolf; daylight that insinuates itself over a windowsill, a few minutes before dawn.

    BEAUTY

Colors matter. Their beauty matters.

The stories of color inform us of each other. Of our elders, whether they be Human, Buffalo, Otter, brush-tailed rock Wallaby, Glacial Stone Ancestors, Alligators. They tell us of the ghosts that once had boys faces, of tomorrow's slain and outraged warriors on the braggartly or owl-eyed (or downright piss-your-pants terrified) night before an impossible-to-win Culloden or Somme, Waitangi or the *sydney cove* of the Eora nation. The howling and keening of dead lad's mothers. The piping of the *baiji* that still murmurs, accusingly, through the raging waters of the Yangtze. Their terrible, terribly loud silence.

The grey and dark of the long arctic twilight.

Fearful that the soot and ash in their hair more often resembles the funeral pyre than the walls upon which their predecessors painted hunt-magic in ochres of blue, grey, red, brown, white. Mr. paint and I settle on *river stone*.

LOSING WHITE

> Portraits hung in empty halls
> Frameless heads on nameless walls
> With eyes that watch the world and can't forget
> Like the strangers that you've met

Zo Damage and I toil to apply the first coat on the first day. The colors we choose to transform a sad, white rectangular cuboid of walls, and odd, eccentric remnant-beams, of Old Growth Forest that has been sliced into lengths of *four-b'-two*, slabs of suspect ceiling, the dead children of primordial red cedar majesty cut into tongue and groove floorboards oh, about a hundred years ago. We transform the breath of this tiny room into the mystery of an ancient cairn of superstitiously threatening menhirs. A secret. A silent space. Almost—but not quite—a confessional.

We use up the entire can on the first go. The following day (I am impatient. No, I'm not, I just know that when a mammal, labouring to push an infant animal from her vagina, quickens, and the head of the unborn crowns, birth is only a matter of moments away. There's no going back) I'm back beneath the streets of Melbourne. A labyrinthine chamber that leads me to treasure. Oops. No, the ground floor, of the temple of bunnings in carlton.

PAINTED PEOPLE

I ride the escalator to the top floor. Where these decisions of great importance are always properly done. The joy, emanating from mister paint as I approach, is palpable. His living ancestor has returned. With the empty can, too, so they don't have to work hard at remembering all the details of our paint-story-in-complicity. This entity has that smile that only a clan fey ever has. A look that colludes. It says *I knew you'd be back. I knew you'd bring the information. Are we both not highlanders? Renegades? Brigands of the north? Of course.* How irreverent of me to even think to ask.

Mr. paint is grandly, splendidly inked. From what I can see, almost as inked as me. Seems that the bunnings middle-management—the *HR cabal*—is not peopled with snobbish, condescending, classist bastards, after all (may the weather gods take that into account at the end-of-days' reckoning).

I guess when your company progenitor was a timber miller from hackney, and you've had generations to thwart the many-cousin'd lairds of the Forests to enable the erection of a pub, an opry house, a slab-full of potentially derelict, worm-eaten falling down houses for the not-so-rich-they-can-afford-stone punters, and a church steeple, or two, like the one just burned down at *notre dame* (oh, you didn't know? Some 1,300 oak trees, from over 50 acres of forest, were murdered and planed into submission in its construction), or like those men-in-charge, incognito and potentially trench-coated, who want to destroy—in Australia—in excess of 260 Trees sacred to the Djap Wurrung peoples, including a traditional birthing tree, that in 2020 were beribboned in readiness for the chainsaws. Their roots to be bulldozed in preparation for a forty-two million dollar upgrade to *the western highway*.

MYTHIC EXCELLENCE

Has this conversation been side-tracked? Not really. We were discussing color. So...

> *The ragged men in ragged clothes*
> *The silver thorn of bloody rose*
> *Lie crushed and broken on the virgin snow...*

Two days ago, the wizard of *genius loci* and I move into the new old house from which I now write to you. A sanctuary of leaning (yes, you read that right). Towards an eventual collapse into the substrata, I am quite sure. I tried sitting at the main side of this table, but I kept sliding precariously toward the kitchen at the end of the hallway. But not before I returned to *that place*.

Yes. Here I am. Once again, in *temple bunnings*, aware that I really do need a sander—as much for an unpolished seal-rib talisman as for the surface of this old worktable—and now the experience becomes positively archetypal in its splendor and artistry.

I hunt for a gold leaf style lacquer, once the appropriate electrical tool has been got, but mister paint is nowhere to be seen. I understand. Once a wayshower has given one of us entrance to the world of specified color, and the choices beyond our often limited imaginations, another must take their place.

And there they are: the child of brightness; the hope of the future.

RAINBOWS

The one who will take up the banner of color in all rainbowedness.

I momentarily forget this most important experience of the land of myth and legend... but then—I do! I am assaulted by joy. A youngster of the post-2016 LGBTQI+ community prances toward me, their eyes still dewy with awareness of that recent, politically-driven (ergo *puerile*) referendum which, had it not passed by the vast majority of even one person, would have seen the two-spirits condemned to a mental ward, banishment, or prison. Under some wigged dude's gavel (do they have gavels in the *old bailey*?) consigning the *buggery act* of 1533 into law, the *sodomy laws* (vague, very vague) of the nineteenth century, into law. The death penalty being reduced to mere life imprisonment instead.

For loving.

And someone thought this was a sane idea?

So, thank you, to the survivors and descendants of *Stonewall*, you are like hobbits overwhelming Mordor! Thank you, *Daughters of Bilitis*; thank you, also, *john gorton*.

This youngster sees me, eyes alight with joy, their strut continuing, their hands in the air, palms towards their own face. Nail polish a majestic silver. I am wide-eyed at the wonder.

I remember you, they say, their look explaining to me that they, too, recognize *my* awareness of *them*; that the last time we exchanged chitchat was the day their fingernails were painted a pale and delicate, aurora borealis green.

New color I see. There is nothing else to say. Words are in the way of a moment's refreshing mutual acknowledgment. Admiration, even. Their fingers wiggle and their head tilts. They grant me a grandchild-wise smile. I want to hug them, but security—the masks-and-social-distancing-bunnings-police—are too close to us. I sigh. They sigh. If mr. paint was here we could sigh collectively, that mutually isolated-sigh that we all need, every now and then.

Now I think I know what you tried to say to me
And how you suffered for your sanity
And how you tried to set them free
They would not listen, they're not listening still

FAMILY

We're born, we exist (sort of, in some instances), we visually stop being who and what we seemed to be. Everything that weaves within the tapestry of these small, vast years is a reason for awe. Your shine. Ours. Me. Theirs. Owners of naught but words and wants.

We all dwell in a humanly-justified world that is chaotically outside of political or comfort-demanded control, like John Cleese or Whoopy Goldberg. Like Hannah Gadsby or donald trump. Like drought and mudslides; meteor strikes and sinkholes.

The species called *us* thinks, seriously much of the time, that it's at the top of some contrived food chain, when the jellyfish in the tidal pool is of the same certainty, and must be correct because they are a single cell, never having received the coded, complex command to self-replicate in incalculable variations! *Excuse me*? They ask of the anthropologist, or cnidologist, if there is such a human researcher. *There is nothing beyond the edge of this briny puddle, so you, you two-legged clever-dick bigot, are deluded. I know. There is only rock and sky and endless sea... Isn't there?*

So what? Ask yourself if you've done all you can to explore the legend of you. To converse and comprehend into some tomorrow we—of the early twenty-first century for lack of a better analogy—cannot imagine. Or can we? Have we?

Living art can be, actually is, who and what we are. The skin we are in. The depths of our humanity and our acknowledgement of kindred with seals, the hunting rights and elder lore of indigenous folk everywhere, the knowledge of Lascaux and the depths of the silver-nailed young bunnings kin. And mr. paint. And some future, as yet unrealized new species of us.

We desire to be acknowledged as being as beautiful as the song.

So, I wish you rainbows, because I've taken the grey.

> *Starry, starry night*
> *Paint your palette blue and gray*
> *Look out on a summer's day*
> *With eyes that know the darkness in my soul*

YEAR ONE CONTINUOUS

(From *Genesis | The Future*)

Skin the color of oak-bark, hair coated in red ochre, faces and hands tattooed with light blue markings, their clothing finely-tanned hide of every hue within nature, gold and other jewelry, horn, bone, wood, shell, and stone, adorning exposed skin, and row upon row of blue clay beads on every proud chest.

A company of heavily armed warriors – of many genders – leap onto huge, shaggy-haired horses and ride towards us, unfazed by the size of our machines, the lead male wearing a red stag pelt, its many-tined horns atop his head, his face and hands tattooed bright blue, his bearing as regal as anyone Sabé has ever witnessed. Beside him is a woman garbed entirely in white, her face, arms and exposed skin a weaving of white clay threads and lines. Her eyes are pale violet, and her hair is alive with serpents of blue dreadlocks, laced with black, hawk-striped and white feathers. She carries a narrow spear with a tip of black metal, sharp and deadly.

'Ursa?' Sabé knows Ursa will be able to communicate. She knows because she's been here before.

Murmurs, from the others in the group about how crazy this is, are ignored. Irrelevant. The pair inputs the code that halts the walkers. They unhook themselves from the data mainframes, undo their protective harnesses and climb down onto, for Sabé, familiar soil.

Both the chieftain in white and the chieftain clothed in a crown of horns, ride ahead of the others, calling their horses to a halt, but they don't dismount.

Ursa holds his hands out, palm up in a universal gesture of friendship.

The chieftain in white slides from the furs of her saddle and comes to him. She places her hands in his and closes her eyes. They moved beneath the lids as though she sleeps and dreams. Then she opened them, the peculiar color almost eclipsed by irises registering surprise.

She gestures to both Sabé and the chieftain to come to her.

In a series of musical notes, throat song and click of the tongue they communicate in a language of animals, reptiles, and birds.

The chieftain in white grunts in appreciation. 'Sabé,' she says clearly. Sabé nods, her hand slipping into Ursa's. The chieftain, the other warriors on horseback and the entire city before them roar in empathy as they link with the matrix, because she knows. The woman out of legend has come to claim the book.

The chieftain dismounts and lifts the great bronze door to the library.

...

Inset lyrics: VINCENT, by Don McLean, 1971.

ONE WOMAN, TEN MEN

Or *stab-your-own-throat-with-a-blade-made-of-dumbness* syndrome.

> *Approximately 2 billion years ago, complex eukaryotic cells, which make up animals, plants and fungi, split from smaller, simpler cells called prokaryotes. Researchers have now identified our closest relatives from before this split.* [1]

INTRODUCTION

I keep company with many cisgender men: sons, friends and colleagues. This story does not refer to them. These people are allies and, in a sense of fairness, some have read this already. They are not the people referred to in *One Woman, Ten Men*. They're cool. Is this a preliminary justification? No. It's to ascertain that you and I are clear. I don't generalize.

A note on the use, or lack thereof, of capitalization, reiterated—

> *We accept with nary a thought that the names of people are capitalized. To write "washington" would be to strip the man of his special status as a human. It would be laughable to write "Mosquito" if it were in reference to a flying insect, but acceptable if we were discussing a brand of boat.*
>
> —Robin Wall Kimmerer

THE MARRIAGE/GOD TRAP

What you see on the news and social media is a metaphorical and actual *herding* of the intelligence of us as a human, flesh and blood animal, down a cliff; down a narrow, railing-less stair into a ravine that seems to have no bottom, evoking a fear that may or may not be advantageous. Oh, I'll mention that fear is not an enemy. Fear is the recognition of a threat that evokes a fight, flight or freeze response. An adrenaline rush that, hopefully, is resolved and dispersed quickly. We are being frightened at this juncture of history, just as we have been over countless hundreds of years, by the premise of a deadly, invisible foe. We are warned that the eradication of freedom could be for our own good.

Now, I do admit to having been smashed with a dog's lead for some child-crime or other, and I also do admit to having lived for a year under the blackboard-eraser-blows of nuns, known as *the children of mary*, at a *sacred heart catholic school* in Sydney, but that rhetoric about an enemy skulking just beyond sight, boogy-manishly, ready to destroy any of us with a menu of potential outcomes, including death, has been around for oh, ages, it seems. And, again, theoretically, as far into memory as the invention of religion. And especially since the idea of a *satan* and *his* unseen, daddy-long-legged, but razor-penised tormentors of flesh and sanctity, deemed demons and imps—*his* minions—that we are threatened will surely inculcate themselves into our nights, under the covers of a single bed, with our hands roaming to where they should not roam.

These little incubi and succubi will have us thinking sulphurous, licentious and uncivilized thoughts, like the ones that warn us that sex is vulgar unless between a man and a woman, and only then when the woman is owned by a man: i.e., married. Just like those nuns who took a vow to be the wives of that poor two thousand year old tortured dead bloke that they get the pleasure of feasting on, sometimes daily, and whose *daddy* figured the brutality of his only son's flesh and blood body was warranted; was *holy*. Something about getting rid of *sin*, despite that having to do with not barbecuing on a sun day, or lusting after your neighbour's cow.

Well, that was a fizzer, wasn't it?

And what is an observational *death*, when *death* (as we consider it) is

the destiny of everyone? And what about the understanding that morbidity is actually the breaking down of the article of life into the varied and differentiated aspects of the whole world? Space stuff. Star refuse: the birth of matter from a speculative *big bang* and the continual transmutation, that is the ongoing process of creative symbiosis, so that where, and if, there is an ending, or a disconnection, it has yet to be realized.

WE SHED THE SKIN WE'RE IN

One of the most imperative arguments for near-future earth is not whether we are headed into another ice age, or what happens if we don't stay in lockdown, or whether a jigsaw of compromised people living on the landmass known, currently, as America (named after Amerigo Vespucci [3], the Italian explorer and originally referred to as the *united colonies* of—), will elect a woman as vice president, or what are the consequences of facial recognition technology on liberty? Will femicide and infanticide continue? Will there be no answer to stopping the debt-, sex, and the abandoned-child slave trade and genital mutilation—of either and all genders. And why is any of this is even up for discussion, rather than realizing it's just straight-out wrong?

How is it possible for the *isms* [4] of prejudice, stereotyping, racism, bigotry, political and religious authoritarianism to even hold purchase on human consciousness? And while I'm on the subject of why—why do we, as a species, talk so much about anything? And just as much about nothing?

DEATH

I recently counted the number of times I have almost died, whether from near-drowning and electrocution to drug overdose, from golden staph after a miscarriage, anaphylaxis from a tick bite, pneumonia from riding a pushbike home from hapkido, in summer, with sopping *gi*, wet with living, messy, organic sweat: water, ammonia, urea, salt and sugar. Truth is, I was never going to die, or I'd be dead. I simply got sick. I was either never close to death, or death has never been far.

To understand this requires a bit of thought. A puzzle, perhaps—

> *A person is standing on a bridge. Then they jump.*
> *When is the moment of jumping?* [5]

—Bernard Casimir,
The Signs of the Times

There is no answer. Person is either on the bridge or they've jumped. There is nothing, not a split millisecond, between being on the bridge and having jumped. This is exciting. We don't know anything. We've just named stuff.

SPECIES DIFFERENTIATION—AN OBSERVATIONAL BEAUTY

We are a species. We are not more important or more sophisticated than any other species. In fact, our capacity to survive at all, considering infant human beings can actually live for years without being able to fend for themselves, proves the concept of superiority laughable. Hierarchy, that is attributed to powerful men with big guns, is actually a thing that chickens do. All considerations of our importance, by media and command, are slanted by a *biblically-induced*, lay-it-on-thick hyperbole. Let's face it, our nearest genetic relatives are, maybe, eukaryotes.

Using words like theorize, speculate, hypothesize, conjecture, guess, imagine and believe allow me to insert question marks into everything I say, in relativity to this topic that would otherwise be cultish and religious. And that is the opposite of what I propose. Hypothetically, then, the microbiome, or gut, of each of us contains ancestral material that we've sucked into our intestinal tracts when we encountered the slide along the theme-park ride of our birth mothers vaginas and... when we took a first breath? We breathed in the entire world. Approximately 2.5 billion years of World, and that a quarter of that same microbiome is Virus.

Spooky? Considering that the human animal population is currently 7,800,000,000 [6], and that it is munching through incalculable herds, shoals and flights of other flesh-and-blood species, is ripping out, decimating, burning, denuding, packaging and distributing every nut, krill, grain of any grass, and forest of diverse other species that (if they could be bothered) also live and perhaps even have rights that have nothing to do with us as a species; so how could we possibly wonder that the virulence of *corona* has decided that now is the ripe season, and that pruning, to thin us out, will rejigger the balance of things?

Why don't we know this? What is all the media hype about? Is it going to end up as a *wrath of god thing*, like HIV-AIDS and the eruption of any volcano, like organised crime and Auschwitz?

> *The ugliest prostitutes specialized in group affairs, passed among several men or even whole squads, in communion almost, a sharing more than sexual. In sex even more than in killing I could see the beast, crouched drooling on its haunches, could see it mocking me for my frailties, knowing I hated myself for them but that I could not get enough, that I would keep coming back again and again*.[7]

—William Broyles, Jr.

Be honest. The world is ending, isn't it? We're utterly fucked, so people better pray, don't you think? We also better listen to the men in charge. Shouldn't we? They've always done the right thing by us, haven't they? Had our best interests? Had our backs? They are made in the image of god, after all, being blokes, aren't they? Yes, we should pray. We are told to. For everything. For an incinerated town, drowned villages, napalmed forests. To stop a riot for justice and equality, for troops that invade independent lands to be safe. We should pray, by god! "Thoughts and prayers," says the prime minister, the president, that *authority*... any authority that considers itself in the know.

THE GOD INSULT

But to what? Or to whom? And when, that we are aware of, historically, have we not been culled? To pray to a supposedly omnipotent deity that is somewhere (but we don't know where), that sees everything and knows everything, but doesn't interfere. An almighty, all-powerful supreme being that even supposedly sanctioned twelve nuclear tests in Australia, sanctioned a government to name a skimpy swimsuit after the nuclear blasting of Bikini island, that considered appropriate the dropping of an atomic bomb on Japan; that led the *shock and awe* attack on modern-day Persia—the so-called cradle of civilization (that just happens to have oilwells), another *Oh, gollygosh, SORRY* outcome. Somewhat ludicrous, eh what? Dare I say that cabal of criminals, at the *council of nicaea*, came up with an idea that is way more than a *tad* paranoid psychotic and burgeoning with self-interest, and enamoured of some romantic nostalgia tied to a decimated city? The lack of logic cracks me up. Because what if god is life? The whole of life? And not an old Greek-looking chap in a white throw-over frock, after all?

We're a species and, in so many ways, and from a subjective point of view, a beautiful one. But why the delusions of significance? Of better-than?

Cacophonous alarm bells at the *oopsies*, at the political photo-op, of a bunch of alpha-pretence-please-don't-look-too-hard-into-my-credentials-faux-cisgender-men, standing around their *Cheshire Cat*, highly dangerous boss cocky, with one lone woman, impeccably blonded, botoxed and dressed in red, a fixed and blindingly-white smile on her face, insisting on their *god-given* sectarianist bullying in the face of an unexpected pandemic, with their pie charts, experts and offerings of "thoughts and prayers?" How are we supposed to outwit a common virus that has danced along the blockchain of the human genome since the long haul of those 2.5 billion years, when the homo-normed, hardwired, straight, suited males of our species, touted as the leaders of the free world, outnumber women by a hundred to one?

How are we going to breed ourselves out of this dilemma and where is the omnipotent deity getting his figures? Or did he/they/it go so mightily crazy around twenty three thousand years ago[8] that women who don't winnow grain, lie on their subjugated backs, wax (an excessively painful affair) every hair off their bodies as though they were parasitically deviant, or people of suspect difference, or opinion-opposition to the rule of clergification, have been chained, tortured, abused, blamed for everything from talking to snakes and plucking apples (*Havah*), to springing fully formed (*Athena*) from a randy olympian bloke's head and not agreeing to him raping not only her but as many nymphs and dryads as could be penetrated [9], or to having creamy, white, seductress thighs (*Maeve*) or wanting to vote in a feudal system that pretends to be a democracy?

NEW AGE SCAMS AND A GODDESS OR TWO

So here we have it. The backstory of this article is a client I worked with last night. This person facilitates workshops on vaginas and things. Stuff about the sacredness of cunt. Her income derives from tantric sex. I have no problem with sex, by the way—tantric or against the wall in a darkened alley—as long as it is consensual and all parties realize the consequences, and shore up their arsenal of condoms against a herpes transmission, or HPV [10] ... yes, still yet more viruses, sexually transmitted, that women and girls need to inoculate against, despite that it is an unsheathed penis that shoots its testicular load deep inside a woman, ejaculating with force enough to embed,

roughly a teaspoon-and-a-bit of semen into the cervical tissue and that allows one lizard-fish-like swimmer of the Amazonian-kind, vaginal river to attain the oddness of transformation.

> *Walk the streets for money,*
> *you don't care if it's wrong or if it's right.*
>
> —The Police, *Roxanne* 1978

The woman on the other side of the computer screen is many hundred miles from me, and yet, with current technology, they are right here in this room. There's a marvel to consider, in difference to the fear of going outside the door without a mask, or disposable gloves (most of which will end up in some turtle's or pelican's gut, slowly strangling their insides with those ear loops and those five empty fingers), but no, we now consider this technology not only normal but our right. The idea of going shopping without the company of a mobile phone—just in case we miss some important message, between the deodorant and the cat food—is provocatively unthinkable.

Her partner has left her. Due to dire financial deficiency, she takes up in the *adult* industry. And because of business her three almost-adult offspring consider her a *something*. What? What has her once-death-us-do-part-spouse said to the people this woman pushed from her pink, mucosal and bloody, but obliging, bodily orifice? That she's a whore? A hooker? A shame? An unacceptable human flesh-and-blood female animal? The two offspring, still dependent on a parent, now live with him. Does she dare not take him to court, for access or custody, for fear someone will expose her as a *hoochi-cooch floozy*? That someone can humiliate her, can accuse her of being incapable of successfully raising offspring because she shags blokes to whom she is almost a stranger? *Good goblins*, she's like a bitch that allows any dog to mount her when she's on heat. But wait. How is this (like an omnipotent deity) also irrational? How is it even a *thing*.

I EXORCISE THEE IN THE NAME OF JESUS CHRIST

This person tells me they think that entities are possessing her, and an egyptian *goddess* is guiding her. Her work in the world is *spiritual*. I ask when she immigrated from the middle east, and what constitutes spirituality. I ask how jerking off a guy's penis is mystically meaningful. I ask how good's the money, and whether she has a secret stash, just in case the need arises and then, what she means by *holy*? She gapes at me, her mouth open, a sheen of sweat and a metronomic tick under her left eye giving her facial appearance a unique individuality and magnificence.

I don't understand you; she says. She throws me a strange line, right then: *I was brought up a jehovas witness*.

OH, is all I say.

JARGON TO CONTROL

This person does not know me.

I was recommended to her by someone else, someone who had a session with me a month earlier. Mostly, nowadays, none of them know me. They are just desperate. And having a rep is probably better than being a celebrity because when someone close to you says, *they're good, they're just not famous*, the person is usually so up for answers to the dilemma of their lives that they'll pay this hidden mystic-whatever-they-are the fee, in kind, for an uninterrupted hour of spotlight, and a series of unexpected and unpredictable future events.

Except... It was said to me, in the year known as 2015 and I had a memoir due for world release, that if *you are not on social media you don't exist.*

If you wanna sell books you have to do the thing.

I did *the thing*. And now I don't do the *thing*. If I still did *the thing* I wouldn't be writing this here, because I would be too busy scrolling to find out how many *likes* the last comments got.

The person on the screen, several hundred kilometres away (as we know distance), thought I would use their language. Thought I would discuss how they could banish entities. Would gasp, in awe, at their unique communication angle with the egyptian personification of an archetype of some unique cred, within the appropriate scene.

Except, I don't.

But because I sit with her, empathizing and sharing information, I care about her. And what she says. And is this, also, a sickness? All this talking? She doesn't stop even though I ask her to, so that I can objectively prophesy her destiny through this wee deck of tarot cards. Is the jargon and self-aggrandisement, occurring with her and the world the media presents to us, the real virus? I never heard of *fake news* before *donaldtrumpism* bought itself a presidency.

To understand requires context. Two things: one is that I used to think the way they do now, but I kept digging into that mountain of contrived and biased *persona-speak* until I found what might—maybe—be some kind of shelf on the way to the bottom of the

Mariana Trench, or more appropriately, on this flesh-and-blood body's expedition to the reunion with rellies, all dancing to the drum of *sister archaea* at *Loki's castle*—one of five hydrothermal vents located at 73 degrees north, on the mid-Atlantic ridge, between Greenland and Norway, at a depth of 2,352 metres—before earth, speculatively, dives into another upheaval.

The other is that the offspring that I bore, adults, have presented me with grandchildren and, as honestly as I know how to be, under the circumstances of communal delusion, I like talking to them. If I said to an eleven year old that I am possessed by entities and guided by an anthropomorphic being that looks like Nefertiti but that is incapable of preventing even one perilous, confrontational drama from unfolding in anyone (that includes *every* species of everyone) they would think what? That I'm telling the truth? That I'm a new age nutter that they have to placate but with whom they can never have an expositional and meaningful relationship? What talks when we talk?

Nothing is true. Everything falls down, composts, fossilizes, turns nova, disintegrates in a second when that bomb goes off, is burned and then, because they will never be able to live like life is presumed to be, live in a post-traumatic-stress-disorder terror and confusion, until the machine is switched off, they are imprisoned, gassed and cremated, decapitated, used as a ball by the Hunza in a polo game as old as time, frozen on the way to *conquering* a mountain crudely named after *george everest* (Chomolungma—pronounced *jo-mo-glang-ma*, translated, by the invaders and destroyers of culture, as *mother*, indigenous to the region), who was a surveyor in the pocket of the now-infamous *east india company*. We're meat. Blood, bone, muscle, viscera, mitochondria. And each of us is host to incalculable families of bacteria, enzymes, viruses, juices, single and multiple cells, organs that can be moved from body to body in a finite manner.

Mortal but immortal.

POSSESSION

All this carry on about a delusional state of breeding. There it is. Seventy thousand dollars on a dress. White. I don't need to tell you that fish are wet. The big day. An official marriage. The daddy (not the mummy; fascinating) walks this girl-woman down the alley of a building, or a garden if it's a nice day, with this audience who are there because... because this day is *important* and requires witnesses and a party, and he *gives her away*. Like a prize cow, or the meat platter after a bingo win or a pub raffle. And she agrees. Suddenly she is no longer her own person. She is a possession. She will usually relinquish her father's name—her ancestral lineage—and take that of the person she marries. Not always, but that's only been slightly popular at the 23:99th hour of the current era.

And here it is. She's destined for a Shakespearean drama of interminably day-to-day, banal but perennially annoying proportions. She doesn't know it yet, because she's bought into the disney *happy ever after* eulogy that never is, and never will be, honest.

> Do you think you are "Indian at heart" or were an Indian in a past life? Do you admire native ways and want to incorporate them into your life and do your own version of a sweat lodge or a vision quest? Have you seen ads, books, and websites that offer to train you to become a shaman? [11]

WARMED BY GREAT EVIL = CELEBRITY

This momentary commentary is just that. Momentary. Because within the blink of an eon I will be countless other species, and who I am, as a human animal, will cease to be relevant, as we understand relevance. The name I am known by means nothing, and neither does *ayers rock* [12], who is Uluru. Naming anything is treacherous because of the packaging. Naming is often done by supposedly exclusive palefaced, Anglo-European invaders and wreakers-of-cultural-havoc. It seems to give us an identity that is so fleeting that even the history books would only record it if we possessed the capacity for great evil on a gargantuan scale. Or because I'm classed, by the fact of genitalia and other assorted bits (like tits, although that's certainly not exclusively female, nor is it always anything other than a silicone bag under a pectoral muscle, after a scalpel slice), as a woman. And a
breeder at that.

You and I are ultimately, superfluous because the records of importances write of men. How many women's faces are on mount rushmore? How many colored, women's faces are on mount rushmore? How many old, tired, wise, *goddessy*, tantric sex workers' identities are carved into the wildness of a mountain, removing mountain-person's uniqueness and superimposing the faces of men of seeming significance.

> *When Rushmore asked a local man the name of a nearby mountain, he reportedly replied that it never had a name before, but from now on would be known as Rushmore Peak (later Rushmore Mountain or Mount Rushmore)* [13]

Will those sculptures still be there in a thousand years? Or will Mountain-Person experience a few Earthquakes that reduce the hubris to rubble, allowing the Ponderosa Pine the dignity of a vastly different thousand years: that of producing offspring?

...

[1] https://www.newscientist.com/article/mg22630204-000-microbes-found-at-bottom-of-ocean-are-our-long-lost-relatives/
[2] Braiding Sweetgrass, Indigenous Wisdom, Scientific Knowledge and the Teachings of Plants
[3] https://www.biography.com/explorer/amerigo-vespucci
[4] Forming nouns with the sense belief in the superiority of one—over another; as racism, sexism, species ism, etc. Forming nouns with the sense 'discrimination or prejudice against on the basis of—'; as ageism, baptism, lookism, criticism, barbarism, darwinism, plagiarism, etc. Sources, several online.
[5] www.thesignsofthetimes.com.au
[6] https://www.worldometers.info/world-population/
[7] https://www.esquire.com/news-politics/news/a28718/why-men-love-war/
[8] https://www.sciencedaily.com/releases/2015/07/150722144709.htm
[9] This reference is a common error that does not take into account the ancient ideas of 'skin walkers' or therianthropy, an animist concept of shape shifting. 'zeus' is likely to be a remnant myth of race or tribe.
[10] human papillomavirus: https://www.cancer.org.au/what-is-hpv
[11] http://www.newagefraud.org/
[12] Uluru
[13] https://www.history.com/topics/us-presidents/mount-rushmore-1

DON'T CAUSE AN EARTHQUAKE

OR: *TAKE YOUR PANTS OFF CAREFULLY*

> *For want of a nail the shoe was lost,*
> *For want of a shoe the horse was lost,*
> *For want of a horse the rider was lost,*
> *For want of a rider the battle was lost,*
> *For want of a battle the kingdom was lost,*
> *And all for the want of a horseshoe nail.*

DREAD, AND I'M IN TROUBLE

Last night I was overwhelmed by dread. Tsunami-like fear. Gut-heavy. About an adult offspring. Are they safe? Are they, unknowingly, consigned to the padded cell of a mental asylum, calling softly *Mummy will come, it's okay, Mummy will come.*

Is this normal? I'm not the only one—I know, because I've sat with you, and tarot, for an hour or more—and *you* know it. You too, without being classified with the brutal and often debilitating dilemma called (because everything has to be categorized, doesn't it) OCD. But many of us, many, many of us/you repeat the same gestures every day. Is it mindless? Am I aware that I do it? Are you aware that *you* do it?

I strip off a pair of trousers, before bed, left leg first. And for the past few weeks, while microscopic critter viruses color our idea of the known world with difference, fear or denial, I've become aware of doing this. Of the exactness of routine. At how I put *just* enough filtered water in the kettle, light a low gas flame, and let the steam relax into the kitchen while I perc the coffee, just in case I've overfilled the bowl that holds the grains, and the brew is bitter. I'll be able to top up the glass of newly-poured coffee with the hot water, you see? Logical.

And on it goes. I'm breaking patterns just now (before heading off to the gym) to write this to you.

Last night I was filled with dread. My breathing shallow. Brutal, gut-twisting. What if...

GEAS

For years I couldn't wear jewelry. If I even attempted to put an earring in one ear the events that followed, even mere minutes later, had me rushing to extract the *tapu* item. That began in 2007. I wrote an article called *The Year the Soul Fled* and posted it online. That year was dreadful, and some of you probably remember. Many of you walked from a demeaning relationship, your mother died, you walked out of a job for no other reason than that you could no longer cope with the fact that the insurance company, that employed you, robs people whose houses burned to soot, and who lost everything of importance to them in the summer bush fires.

2007

An acquaintance of a few years moved into where I was living in 2007. I thought nothing of it, except to allow them space to recover from a partner of a few years who was talking them to death. Sure, they drank quite a lot of red wine, and occasionally embarrassed themselves, and made other people feel uncomfortable when they fell over on the concrete; laughing because they'd broken the side of their face when they smashed into a telegraph pole and were, consequently, embarrassed, had the cops searching, after their pantyhose and handbag were delivered to us by a scared and bewildered stranger who lives three blocks away... but hey, they're a friend. You put up with stuff like that when you care.

What had that to do with the *seemingly* OCD certainty that if I popped a bangle on my wrist the world might end? Everything.

Fast forward nine years and I'm living with a mage (a friend of forty years) here in Melbourne. And that same broken person who moved in with me back in 2007 when I stopped being able to wear jewelry in case I killed someone I love, is also here. They are now dying from the indolence of alcohol and a lack of the need to work for their supper or anything else—not that they seemed to need to eat at all, really. Or are they already dead but still animate? When do we really know which is which? I take them to hospital, despite protestation, because they won't live another day. All their organs are shutting down. They are a 34 kilogram condescending, arrogant, violently ill, impossible drunk... friend... A forty seven year old, once beautiful human being, now stale and, really, shredded and smashed of shine.

And the curse lifted. The person who came home from that hospital was not the same person who had been a friend. Does that make sense? That friend died. This is a doppelganger. A *golem*. What has that to do with trouser legs, earthquakes and jewelry?

    EVERYTHING.

I *knew*. Do I have to explain what is impossible to explain? That I had been complicit in their death? I had, you know. I had chosen not to judge their behavior because I'm nice that way. There's a *but*, and here it is: If we don't judge we're crazy.

I am slathered, now, in ornamentation: the kind I like. The weird and the cravenly exotic. The blatantly and personally mine. And nothing. No one dies, no world tipping inexorably towards a wobble, no sun going nova. Oh, wait... Lore, stop it. That has nothing to do with your turquoise 20 mm earlobe plugs, and now, when I'm going to bed at night I pull off the trousers, left leg first. I've tried doing it the other way, thinking *be flexible, c'mon!* but that was only one night's rebellion.

HOWEVER

Most of you are aware that I foretell the future, and you all understand how spooky that is, and how seemingly-impossible, but that it works and is real and, as one of this person's son's—an absolute pragmatist and anti-theist—is prone to say, *Yeah, all religion is lame, but what is tarot?*

Last night I was in a miasma of dread. Is it the oil spill in Mauritius? The uprising in Belarus? The blast in Beirut? Corona doing her death dance in Mexico? An Aboriginal child being slammed behind stark metal doors: another *black death in custody* that this government is probably annoyed about because the news of such disturbs their snorting of that extra-special line of imported cocaine? Is that adult kid of mine really in a padded cell, calling for me in a delirium of uncontrolled psychosis? They don't answer their phone, so who knows?

THE BUTTERFLY EFFECT AND CHAOS THEORY

The Butterfly Effect? Earlier during that same day I'd stitched a talisman into a dreadlock. An old thing. A spiral of carved bone. As the anxiety roiled wisdom's guts, I finally took the scissors and, in defiance of any *OCDness*, I cut off the offending item. Instant relief. Fear gone. I'd fixed it.

Before you think, *Oh well, there goes the relationship I thought I had with this favourite tarot reader*, just remember, or consider, whether or not the smallest thing anyone—human—does that deviates from a

norm (because most... all... other species don't deviate unless they are in spontaneous evolution) *does* cause an earthquake. This is one earth. ONE EARTH. And everyone/thing/every, everyone/thing is conjured from when we discovered we could orbit a sun. We just differentiated; you see? We owe consciousness and awareness to that, not some irrational and probably perverse deity, invented by that council of nicaea, supposedly omnipotent so what, then, is it *doing* causing the sixth mass extinction and the disposable face mask, and not informing us that it's a bio-hazard?

STORM RAVAGE

It used to be thought that the events that changed the world were things like big bombs, maniac politicians, huge earthquakes, or vast population movements, but it has now been realized that this is a very old-fashioned view held by people totally out of touch with modern thought. The things that change the world, according to Chaos theory, are the tiny things. A butterfly flaps its wings in the

Amazonian jungle, and subsequently a storm ravages half of Europe.

—Terry Pratchett and Neil Gaiman, *Good Omens*

Tarot is the art of interpreting patterns. I use a well-thumbed pack of cards. Do I read patterns in everything? Yes. The older I get the better I get. That's annoying, by the way, and I've almost learned to shut up about it, but give me a kellogg's corn flake box and I'll tell you what you don't know. It's that overwhelming at times. I'm ragged in crowds, even personal book launches.

I was on the phone, a week ago, to the wife of someone I'd never met, but who is related to me through a so-called father I have, also, never met (for another story, yes there is one. A freedom story). Her husband (84 years old) was in the background. He didn't want to speak to a person like me. What did he call me? A fruit loop. Ah, yes, the name-game used to humiliate those of us who are considered "different".

Then, I had a typical bolt out of the blue and said, *Who's the smoker? Lung cancer. Now. Today. Death, good buddy. Sorry for the loss.*

Profound silence. Then the woman said, *Nobody.*

After another ten seconds she said, *Oh god...*

Again, I waited. *My sister died a year ago today, of lung cancer. From smoking.*

I had the old man's attention in the background (I was on speaker).

What else do you see, he mumbled, unsure of his sarcasm now.

An older man, I answered, *with a blonde moustache stained at the bottom by tobacco. He's got a riding crop in his hand and I smell horses.*

Well, that was his father, who, yes, was a horseman out back of Bourke. He had a photo of his grandfather, also, who looked the same, but who had died at the battle of Beersheba, in 1917. He was of the 4th Light Horse Brigade. That went on for an hour. It was like watching an inner movie, and it turned him from being a nasty, misogynist old ratbag to a deeply implicated conversationalist. Not that I wanted him in this current life, so I excused myself from the call and, half-jokingly, said to the old guy, *You owe me $150.*

Is there a moral to this story? Yes. Don't be afraid to be right. As long as you do no harm (that you intend, or that you know of) you can accept being meticulous. You can turn the key in the lock seventeen times. You can check on the hens at 3 a.m. when there isn't a sound because... if you didn't, and Goanna *does* get in, you'll slap yourself next morning when all the women lay dying in what you thought was a safe, secure chook house.

...

FERAL: REWILDING LANGUAGE

I was given the casket on the condition I disposed of it in the deepest, most secure underland site that I reached – a place from which it could never return. The second of the objects was an owl cut from a slice of whalebone. It is a talisman and what it connotes is magic. The minke whale from which the owl was taken had washed up dead on the shoreline of a Hebridean island.

—Robert Macfarlane, *Underland*

INTRODUCTION

Disclaimer: the names and situation associated with the woman called Hecate are fictitious. Any resemblance to anyone living or dead is purely coincidental. The scenario, however, is based on a factual, similar event.

"I'm a witch," said Hecate, smiling that smile I've seen countless times before. "I've read your book. It really helped me center myself after my divorce."
"Which book?" I suck on a cup of coffee, blissed at the autumn sun despite the intuitive hackles.
She's confused, as though I've just devoured a baby in front of her.
"Witchcraft Theory and Practice. Um…"
"You didn't know I'd written more?"
"Ah, no. It's great, by the way!"

I'm due to facilitate a multi-week workshop, called *Feral*, on the rewilding of language, beginning next saturn-day. I don't want strangers hanging about this house. Have I had death threats in the past? Yes. I'm still alive though. Obviously. I prefer to meet those I don't already know in a café downtown. Suss 'em out, inoffensively, obviously.

"No, it's not," I respond, kindly. "I signed the contracts with the publisher, for that book, in 1998."
"Classic!"
We're getting on nicely, so far. Am I about to fuck that up? Of course.
"So, you're Greek?"

She's forty nine. I remember being forty nine. All the kids grown and gone their own ways. Me thinking I knew everything. Silly stuff like that. Her hair is dyed a precocious and eye wateringly fluorescent pink, and a really lovely septum piercing dangles above her top lip. She keeps fiddling with it. She's as wildly bohemian as any goth on the streets of Melbourne and I'm mightily respectful, if not a bit wary. She wears a rustic, heavily tarnished silver pentagram, and her fingernails, while fake, are killer-black and as close to talons as a nail parlor can get em.

"Hecate…" I continue. "Myth and legend and all that. You don't look Greek."
"I'm not. I'm Australian. Hecate is my witch name."
"I'm dreadfully sorry about that book, then."

PART 1 – WHAT'S IN A NAME?

Naming is treacherous…

It's time we had this conversation. And Hecate, the woman sitting with me, is a powerful case in point. She is not who she thinks she is, and I am about to become involved in her true-life mystery, and a magic that is both real and tactile. But first you and I have some talking to do.

Witchcraft, as an action. Witchcraft is something one does. Witchcraft is often equated with wicca, and wicca is referred to with an upper-case W, to indicate its importance as an entity in the modern parlance, in the illusionary, non-place, called the *west* (west of what, I am unsure. It's a rather silly construct) and wicca is, currently, considered a valid religion.

WICCA

But wicca is not witchcraft; is not specifically draíochta, and does not, of itself, denote the work of druids. It is a ritualized, quite new, devotional practice that I was involved with for many decades but that, ultimately, being a savage, a pedant *and* an anarchist, I came to understand as a magnificent, utterly well-intentioned form of religion where dualisms and invocations take the place of hopes and prayers. I realize I am repeating an earlier chapter, by the way. I'm not that old.

Douglas Ezzy's writing [1] confirms Hume's hopes for the future. That work, published six years later, is essentially a collection of testimonies: fifteen chapters in which sixteen practicing pagans (including Ezzy) speak of how the practice of paganism has affected their lives. The tone is warm and conversational, and the pagans emerge as charming and interesting people, ranging from youth to late middle-age. Common themes include the feeling that the christianity of their upbringing did not fit their view of the world; the electric experience of working ritual alone and in a group, a concern with both feminism and the environment, and the celebration of human life, from birth to sex to death.

I am fey with ceremony: fires on the hill, smouldering sap of spruce, the need for an uncluttered space, outheld hands, shadow, talismans and charms, a gesture-stick etching sigils in sand or soil; or cellar dust. The list is long, and many are the commercial outlets that will provide us what we *seem* to need, that are none of the above, to enable us to be well-prepared to function within the ideal parameters of some *chosen way*. To sell us stuff that, according to the books, is appropriate for *witches*. To authorize meaning.

Because, Hecate-forbid, to work ceremony in jeans, socks and a woolly jumper is plain, well, *plain*.

SPELLS PART 1

People often write to me asking for a spell for this-or-that. Some claim to be cursed. Some ask for the cure for fear, or as a way to get rid of someone, or to find love. To attract a job or evoke world peace. Do they work? See SPELLS PART 2, as I'm about to get distracted by the other side and its use of word magic (or, in the case of the *synod of Whitby*, "a hostile sword" quote is from Bede) to utterly change the course of human thought.

Thus...

> What must it be, then, to bear the manifold tortures of hell forever? Forever! For all eternity! Not for a year or an age but forever. Try to imagine the awful meaning of this. You have often seen the sand on the seashore. How fine are its tiny grains! And imagine that at the end of every million years a little bird came to that mountain and carried away in its beak a tiny grain of that sand. How many millions upon millions of centuries would pass before that bird had carried away even a square foot of that mountain, how many eons upon eons of ages before it had carried away all.
>
> —James Joyce, on *hell*.

NEVER BOAST, NEVER THREATEN

Magic has its perks because there's no overt threat involved. To anyone or anything. Despite the bad rap. But *hell*? It took zarathustra to invent that and, a millennia or so later, zealots of the cult of the dead god to use it to threaten small children, sensual women, anyone with an alt-sexuality that's anything not bogun,

Trump oppositionists, child-sellers and/or dying soldiers, those in the path of the hurricane or of those, in parched and arid landscapes (because the cotton-growers vampired a river), begging for rain.

This is not it. Where is the wisdom in any of it? And if there is none—almost a need to coerce and prove oneself alternatively worthy—why is the practice (or the idea) still adhered to, even after a hundred years of blatant propaganda and, also, sincere, if deluded, claims of authenticity? Like christianity, even buddhism, that offers the adherent an afterlife of vague cloud-and-right-hand-of-godness, terror—that mountain-pecking-birdiness, that is hell—or some flight into the body of a newborn someone or something.

But what has this got to do with witchcraft? And when did the word become a being thing instead of a doing thing? Have I been down the road of claiming? Yes. Did I know I'd bought into a cult, like any of the above? No. Did it gain me notoriety? Yes, but mainly in the minds of people who've never met me. Who are looking for a mirror within in which to see themselves. I understand that. Because there is a *ness*. A *something*, that implies that witchcraft is, well, witchcraft.

But "a witch?" *Houston, we have a problem* (and yes, I know that's a meme) or, in this case, *Hecate we have a problem*.

SECTARIANISM, FEAR AND SPLINTER CONFORMITY

—BACKSTORY

The early era of when a spotlight was actually claimed by an individual, rather than media, or theocratically-imposed rhetoric was in the latter part of the 1960s. Prior to its romp towards acceptability, in the form of wicca, witchcraft was not even considered a *something*, outside of the mind of men, religion, the church, particularly peeved women, pulp fiction and b-grade movies.

Witchcraft has maintained a waft about it, in populist consciousness, of a dirty little bitter woman-face of dumbness, and hysterical, disease inducing scandal. The foul and uneducated scowls of old women, with crooked backs and single eyes, living deep in forests, eating children who have become lost, or else, if in positions of prominence, within a highly christianised and suspect society, the secret queen of the castle dungeons, holding center stage, naked or slightly-so, albeit grandly draped, in a position of power and displaying an ornate, mysterious garter, endowed by the attending acolytes and adherents, who wantonly lust after her alter-prone flesh-and-blood body whose spread legs temporarily encase whichever man is considered sufficiently well-represented within the court of kings, the crimson choir cassock of a papal cardinal, or the top hatted, moustached and monocled among the monied 1%, the aristocratic, the nobled or merchant-membered of a popular *east India trading company* equivalent (in the twenty first century) like *bhp*, *goldman sachs* or the *epsteinian* uberclass.

These images, and fetishes were, and often are, food for the media and the *mcdonalds*-minded. Or else, particularly in the new diadem of defamation, *disney-ness*.

Tacitus, book XIV, states –

30: On the beach stood the adverse array, a serried mass of arms and men, with women flitting between the ranks. In the style of Furies, in robes of deathly black and with dishevelled hair, they brandished their torches; while a circle of Druids, lifting their hands to heaven and showering imprecations, struck the troops with such an awe at the extraordinary spectacle that, as though their limbs were paralysed, they exposed their bodies to wounds without an attempt at movement. Then, reassured by their general, and inciting each other never to flinch before a band of females and fanatics, they charged behind the standards, cut down all who met them, and enveloped the enemy in his own flames. The next step was to install a garrison among the conquered population, and to demolish the groves consecrated to their savage cults: for they considered it a duty to consult their deities by means of human entrails. — While he was thus occupied, the sudden revolt of the province was announced to Suetonius.

It was from the voices and pens of the purportedly recently vindicated, that a hypothetical modern magical practitioner spat *I am here, and I will claim a tax break.*

Without going too deeply into the repeals by the British commonwealth, I will draw your attention to a law passed in 1735 and called *the witchcraft act*, that changed (slightly) its veil of godliness in 1951 to become the *fraudulent mediums act*. These mothballed condemnations allowed for the emergence, into a public domain, of Gerald Gardner, a bloke sprung from the cabals of nineteenth century elitism—well-traveled to places considered the antithesis of an entrenched and self-certain christianity, such as Ceylon, Malaya and Cypress—and a family made rich by the timber trade, to become a member of a *rosicrucian* cult (circa 1930), practicing—or so I spae—out of Christchurch (in Dartmoor, not the Aotearoa one), the territory of the invader/colonizer Saxons, who referred to the place as *tweoxneam*, and that was stolen or misappropriated from an hypothesized indigenous Celtic tribal affiliation known as the *Dumnoni* [2] – *Deep Valley Dwellers*, in a land of mists and mystery, once covered in Oak forests.

> The following legends show a progression from giants to witches to pixies and, of course, the Evil One also makes an appearance. Naturally there are also ghost stories.

> —dartmoor.gov.uk
> Dartmoor Legends

EMPIRE

Was gerald gardner's fascination with the folklore and indigenous practices of other cultures his reason for consorting with the figure of the rich English woman he coined as "old dorothy clutterbuck",

and whom he claimed initiated him into a coven in the New Forest, England? He certainly had his days of notoriety: claiming a philosophy degree from a suspect American consortium. [3]

> *In 1910 he was initiated as an apprentice freemason into the Sphinx Lodge No. 107 in the British occupied Colombo (then Ceylon), affiliated with the Irish Grand Lodge (the leader of which was a member of what is known as the hellfire club). Gardner placed great importance on this new activity...*

> —Wikipedia, *Gerald Gardner*

STOP NOW

That's enough of that. Gardner, valiente, crowley, leadbetter, blavatsky, budapest, simos and, eventually, (at the small-scale end of this) me. We have all perpetuated (and in some instances, still do) our own brand of misappropriation and, even now, in the era of social media, we can add the coagulant diatribe of multiple religious, anthropological (indigenous and/or conspiratorial) constructs to the mix.

So, to unravel. To finally stop. Because the sectarianist mine-is-realer-than-yours-ideological inventiveness, and fiction, has reached an inevitable dead end. Why? All are based on figment, guesswork, desire, theatre and, at the core, deceit, on both sides of a suspect righteousness and equality debate. Wicca is a *fuck-you-I-won't-do-*

what-you-tell-me [4] snub of orthodox behavioural demands by people with intentionally thin lips. So far, so great, but wait...

The indescribable lostness of a usurper people-animal, has condemned the softer voices of near-extinct environments, cultures and species to derogatorily-penned *fauna*, non-European indigenous languages to brute-speak that we, as an Arctically-pale-bodied human multi-product supermarket aisle of societies, unable to justify our own inadequacies, are determined not to care about. Until late in the twentieth century (and probably even now—I'm such a fucking optimist) our fore-parents were, and are, hoping they can pretend to ignore the voices of terror and the crash/boom of calving ice that is now ominously and inevitably raising sea levels, to the degree of drowning small, inhabited Pacific islands, while those hiding behind wealth and mental instability (unfortunately continuously) rape and plunder, bomb and poison, as companies, corporations and governments have done throughout recorded history, where resides all that does not conform to this netted, gilded desire for more of n... (insert something).

The above practices are now, in *politikspeak*, called *free trade*. Is this in the vain hope that the word "free" will act as a blue pill [5] for all this plastic, and all these oil and chemical spills, deforestation and destruction of biodiversity and habitable non-structures, unparalleled, aberrant soil degradation and river-killing? All the smiley-faced conspiracy theorists, lower down on the hierarchical pyramidal diagram, many of whom remain utterly caged in the zoo, who suggest the wealthy drink the blood of human babies in ritualized debauchery, to... to what? To enable the accumulation of more? To grant eternal life? To appease the deity that abrahamic theocrats have conveniently termed *satanic* because no, *they* don't drink the blood of a man who died, mercilessly, sort of like anybody the *master race* deems problematic, every sun day, sometimes even daily, because he/they held/hold the keys to the previously alluded-to cage?

All while awaiting all the dead to rise up, as was once upon a time promised (because that tortured, murdered man didn't really die, he just ascended. To where, some of us are yet to imagine, because, as the late, great John Lennon once sang "Above us only sky...") in all their flapping, grey skinned, eyeless and lipless, forested world of Proteobacteria, Pseudomonas, Firmicutes, Peptoniphilus and Clostridium [6], like something H. R. Giger will only ever dream of. Are we, as a society historically drenched in the blood of collusion, in genocide and slavery, replete with a colonialist, destructive and overtly fundamentalist ideological attitude, going to continue to claim a radicality that is, if honest, the binary offshoot of monotheism?

Are we, as supposed anarchist, heretical radicals who refuse to kneel before the symbol of torture, in an ostentatious building owned by the governments of a deeply flawed patriarchal, misappropriated spin, actually perpetuating the same pomposity, but with a twist that sticks its tongue out at daddy, in a gesture that says *fuck you*, that is mere posturing because we have nothing better, wiser or unfettered to leap onto and claim?

Well—

    SPELLS, AGAIN

50/50—JOLLY GREAT ODDS, WOT?

That's your chance of having a spell work. No matter how many candles are carved and shaved with some form of *boline* or other, no matter how many letters from the *tetragrammaton* one writes with the blood of your pinkie, whether in sigils-in-clay, carved onto dubious Hebrew-tinged rosicrucian amulets, hung about the bed of a newborn, to repel *demons*, or onto a runic, or ogham-like birch, hazel or rowan branch (perhaps an oak one—although that's just a radical and uneducated guess at specificity; oh, lambs-to-the-slaughter, I sound like I'm serious) stripped of bark and tied at each end with red thread, sealed with black sealing wax bought for this explicit purpose and, once passed through the smoke of incense, is buried in the back yard with a *so mote it be* as the spade is put away. Whether one entombs a cat behind the chimney bricks, buries a boot under the paving stone of the family home or fills a jar with urine, bent nails and hair from an enemy's shower stall plug hole that is, once chanted over, consigned to a cemetery plot or a building site where the concrete is due to be poured in a week because one has done one's research about this.

I have been part of the running-away-from-home movement, loosely called *paganism* (a word I emphatically dismiss because I am not Italian... although I do seem to have a thin green line of ancestral DNA along the fault line of the Tiber) for several decades. On the downhill slide away from same, for several more. If spells worked, every woman in the *miss universe* pageant, asking for a wish to come true, would have made world peace happen. So would *christmas*, with its *peace on earth, good will towards all men* chauvinism. But they don't. And, by dungeons and chains, why would any sane person summon love from an individual who doesn't? Why would one lay healing hands on a person whose destiny it is to die today?

ARE ALL SPELLS SELFISH?

What about the woman who comes to me asking me to work a spell to stop her daughter being raped by her own uncle, because the police couldn't/wouldn't do shit when the child says nothing, and medical examinations are inconclusive? Well, I am certainly going to piss in a vegemite jar for that, and add a few bent nails and broken mirror shards. Because the alternative would land me—&/or the mother—in jail for first degree murder, despite the abused child's silence for fear of consequence.

SO, WHAT *IS* WITCHCRAFT THEN?

Truth is, there is nothing definable about it. The being, knowing practitioner of a something that *could* be classed as witchcraft is not going to say. If they do, they are boasting and, while I have no problem with boasting per se, I do have a problem with *The Complete Book of Spells, Ceremonies and Magic*, and every other book on a similar trajectory (a wall) that I gave up exploring thirty years ago.

The equivalent word—almost the anathema of the word *witchcraft*—is *miracle*. A seemingly supernatural outcome to a threatening or doleful experience that cannot be considered 'normal' or 'predictable'. Being found alive, in the rubble of a bombed out neighbourhood, in Syria, eleven days after the buildings were turned to ash and debris, stunned and confused but otherwise unscathed. How is that possible? It isn't, apparently. Therefore, it is a *miracle*. A "wondrous work of God" [7]. No thanks to the audacious will to live that many, many species continue to display, despite all the vain and economically-sanctioned cruelty we, as a human animal, can inflict, just because we think we're better.

...

THE DEVIL IS REAL,

AND IT'S ON THE 6 O'CLOCK NEWS

Or FREEDOM OF SPEECH? IN WHOSE WORLD?

> *To live in delusion is to live in the comfort of ideology.*
>
> —John Ralston Saul,
> *The Unconscious Civilization*

I remember them the night before a big hunt. The old women dressed in antlers and skins still hung with polished hooves, singing the songs to summon the herd, dancing the dance of the species whose garments they wore. Invoking wind and weather and the voices of ravens, to tell of the run come daylight. Down below the snow line. Through eerie fog, and foot-deep snow that says nothing. Startling at the crack of high branches blowing in an invisible wind. An endless forest of ash and spruce and birch.

Descending the cliff face, following a waterfall frozen in time, to the valley and out onto the plains. And here they come! Vying with wolves, the hunters begin the long lope as the vast herd tears up ancient sod and strikes sparks off cleared granite where the sun has melted the thinner freeze to hoar slush. Spears are black lines against a white sky, taking down an adolescent buck. Him dropping dead from one shot, perfectly aimed, that pierces deeply to within muscle and organs just behind the foreleg. Into the heart. The hunters gut him, thanking him for being the one. Honouring him. The hot liver is bitten, first by the hunter that made the kill and then shared. The intestine is emptied, its innards left for crows and ants and whoever else lives close enough to smell the blood.

— Ly de Angeles and Melaine Knight,
The Skellig, a Shapechanger Tale

HIDDEN IN PLAIN SIGHT

I recently had a solar keratosis (a lump, puppies, a cancer) removed from an eyelid. How is that newsworthy? Well, it isn't. But I have a long habit of asking people for their stories, and really meaning it. The person treating me grew up somewhere in modern Africa. The offspring of christian missionaries. Did they live in indigenous accommodation? No. They also had nothing to do with the provision, albeit unintentionally, of Kalashnikov AK 47 assault rifles, with which to either defend *their* lands or kill off the last white rhino, the head of which would be taxidermized, sold and hung from the wall of some CEO in a pretence that he was some great white hunter *inkosi*.

Or did they? Do any of us, who are so-called palefaced and privileged (that's a person who lives in a dwelling with running water) contribute to the expansion of the need for such weaponry? Of course, we do.

PROTEST THAT SAVAGE LOSS OF FREEDOM

Then, today, I hear tell of several protests, for and against stuff, that are happening in Melbourne. Appreciated. Thank you. Can you please put your used facemasks in a specially provided *contaminated biohazard disposal unit* instead of chucking them in the gutter? Because around here, in the north of Melbourne, that's what you're doing. And the gloves.

The snitching on a neighbour, or calling the cops because a jogger is walking and has his mask down, well, that's not new, is it?

SEX AND THE CITY

I also scrolled through all of the article by Mandy Nolan, called *Monsters Are Real*, and the belated Marie Claire on *Gag Laws*.

And this happened when? In some lost age?

The point is: what we don't know. What we are distracted into forgetting. What don't we know? And does it matter? While we're at it, what do we *think* we know, in difference to the personal experience of N..., (fill in the gap).

I watched an online interview between a colleague and a *qanon*-inspired interviewer, on the conspiracy of *covid 19* and connotations to new world orders, reptilians and satanism, so here I go, about all of it. *Sitchen* stuff. *Icke* codswallop. Fear, with an ego and an appetite for adulation and royalties, but that has no answer; only the glee of blame without recourse to a solution that is not final. Blokes over forty who are pissed that they're not Keith Richards. Conspiracy is the only salt amongst the ineffectual, it seems. Fascinated with violation and baby sacrifice.

Comment of the day... PUUUUURRRLEASEEEEE!

STANDING ROCK AND THE PILBARA

Are we so young we forget Nagasaki? Maralinga? The Marshall

Islands and Muruoa? Are we so naïve that we no longer think intergenerational trauma for the erasure of Indigenous culture and language is nothing anymore? That it's in the past? That the invasions, the persecutions, the genocide perpetuated on SO MANY is old history?

The WA Government granted approval to destroy dozens of sites just days after Rio Tinto destroyed 46,000-year-old rock shelters at Juukan Gorge in the Pilbara [1].

And tell me we have won the right to elect anyone. That *they* have a right to lie to us. Read this and advise me we have rights at all. Read this and explain to me why the young man I sat on the pavement with, on swanston street, who had achieved a phd in physics, is begging?

I'm suggesting that whatever our potentially bigoted views on education, capitalism, corporal punishment, are the slagging of the #metoo, #blacklives matter #indigenouslivesmatter hashtags, law and order, and believing the *dream* of owning one's own home and the sprouking of *make dreams come true* could actually be the real terror.

The offense of presumed privilege.

We have not been, and are not being, educated.

The world of human beings, according to several activists, is being schooled and not educated.

And we wonder at *monsanto* and the huge, unprecedented agriculture industry but... somehow consider that we have a green light to do this. We need our *maccas*! Our *deliveroo* "food freedom" [2], our plastic-wrapped diet lockdown relief...

> "Food freedom" aims to make Deliveroo more accessible while maintaining a fun tone of voice. Because it delivers from restaurants, the brand is typically seen as a more expensive option compared with businesses such as Just Eat. The campaign's idea is to spotlight the happiness that comes from the freedom to get food however and whenever you want it – whether that is ordering a meal on a hungover saturday or to fuel a late night at the office.
>
> —Deliveroo advertisement

NOT ABOUT ME

I'm not telling a personal story. That's too big an *ask*. And those of you who read *Initiation*... I wrote that book for you. Is it about me? No one remotely intelligent exposes their own underbelly to the public. Not without a right-proper stipend for the storyteller. I wrote it so that our mother's mothers, and all they strove for regarding their idea of independence and equal rights, are not forgotten. What had to happen on mon days. The beatings that were condoned by *rule of thumb*. The children who were told to shut up when they complained about the local priest... the courts and the governments that did—and still do—condone the violent sexual aberrations of privilege.

I was brought up with one of many sayings. "Ha," prophesies the milkman, overhearing a conversation between two women about how bad the recession is biting into their businesses; their weekly pocket money handed to them by the husband—the man of the house—don't get me started. "Ya get the same pattern, historically," he informs them, "a boom, a bust, then a war." And he repeats it: "A boom. A bust. A war."

We might wish he wasn't right but then, if wishes were horses beggars'd ride, eh?

While we complain about a lack of freedoms, to gather at a pub or a funeral, or a footy match, child slavery statistics explain that more than 100 million children will still be trapped in child labour by 2020 [3] and that girls and women are forced into the debt of the slave trade, and sex trafficking at the rate of, oh, I dunno...

> *Worldwide, false promises are ways in which traffickers bait and enslave their victims – both adults and minors. Indigenous populations and those who live in abject poverty are typically economically and politically marginalized; thus, most lack rights and access to basic services such as education which make them particularly vulnerable to sex trafficking.*
>
> —endslaverynow.org

THE SHAME OF RENTING

I think I understand the need for roadblocks. People from the city who want to go fishing, or just get out, so their kid's asthma doesn't kill them because someone, apparently, is using up all the intubation in the overwhelmed hospital system... but why the $5,000 fine, per person, in every car, heading south or west or north? Why is this money grab on? Who, by the almighty bloody fuck, would risk that kind of a fine to get their kids some fresh air? Would they be the same people who tried to see Grandad before he died, a mere month ago? What kind of government thinks this is an acceptable form of revenue raising? What does it portend?

I don't want to be the bearer of doomish drivel, but I—at almost 70 years residing in this flesh-and-blood-body, am being demanded of, by life, to once again open these eyes, while I still can. To not turn away. To know that Melbourne, New York, Buenos Aires, Paris and London can become West Papua or Krakow, without us even noticing.

Until the trucks come.

Until the loading and dispersal "for our own protection". Until the forced inoculations, or the forced sterilization (oh, wait, that last one is old news).

I live in a big old house. I rent. I have always been suspicious of debt, and the construct of ownership. Am I safer than those who went into unrealized bondage? *Badgers and bull ants*, not if it was 1929, or 1987, 2008 or… well, again. But wait!

    FUNNY CAT VIDEOS

I don't want to wreck your saturn day (or whatever day you read this), but I think we need to remember what we *think* does not exist. To remember that the color of our hide does *not* always protect us, and that yes, we need to fear.

I wasn't going to talk with you about this this, but I have a voice and I'm not in a gulag yet (I think they're about to be built, and be called *quarantine centers*).

Or am I?

'Mummy, can you tell me the Snow White story again?'

Molly tucks the wild, pale-haired, albino daughter Baron, into the covers on the bottom bed, her pet white rat curling around her young shoulders like a winter stole, her brother Jonathan peering over the edge of the top bunk, thumb in his mouth. Molly thinks they should be the other way around, him being only three, Baron being eight, but she thrusts away the self-deprecating thought, knowing they'd just wait for her to leave the room anyway.

She reaches for the heater under the window and dials the thermostat up as much as everyone's allowed to do, so the power doesn't go off.

Outside is dead still but that's not a promising sign. It's a very frightening sign. With temperatures this low, people are going to die more than usual. Particularly with the energy grid being so erratic. It hasn't been this cold in recorded history. For over a decade the weather has become more and more unpredictable. The winters more savage, the summers melting the tarmac at airports preventing flights, and dropping planes right out of the sky. Molly won't even risk taking them all to visit Tom's family for Christmas next week. Baron and Jonathan are both sad about that, but what's worse?

Tom's working at the uranium mines across the other side of the world, on Kata Tjuta country. A place called Kakadu. So, during the holidays, it's up to Molly to keep her and the kids safe. And the animals. To prevent Jasper, their big lolloping hound pup, and Baron's white rat Robert-son-of-Rudolf, from going outside and maybe freezing to death or getting hit by some maniac skidding their car on the black ice. Because people are still crazy, risking the drive home like they are doing, the sky green as licorice and heavy with this impending, terrifying Arctic ice vortex. The roads slippery where you can't see it, electricity wires snapping in silent death, and the internet all but useless, satellites off-course and malfunctioning.

'You warm enough?' Molly pretends she's happy, when both the kids know it's not true. She inherited her empathy and the telepathy from her own mother, dead now these past six years. Dead... Now that's an odd thought, Moly realizes, because she hears her mother in her mind every day. A ghost or something...

I'm asking you to talk. In person. To the people who will listen. Quietly.

[1] https://www.abc.net.au/news/2020-09-17/bhp-gives-evidence-at-juukan-gorge-inquiry/12672628
[2] https://www.campaignlive.co.uk/article/deliveroo-goes-global-oddball-ad-campaign-celebrating-food-freedom/1523946
[3] https://www.unicef.org/csr/child-labour-portal_more.html

FRAGILE

A man's mother died, and when she was well-buried he went about disposing of her things. Emptying her house. Making it ready for a sale. Her? She'd arrived after the *second world war*, from Europe, a refugee, a voiceless woman. She got married. She gave birth to this boy currently erasing her. She hummed while cleaning, or washing, or shopping, or she put on the telly and sat silently staring at its endless consumerist conning. She baked *palačinky* or *deruny* (she learned to knead the dough for the pastry before what happened, happened), she got fat, grew whiskers, got old, wore slippers to the corner shop, ignored the cat, was forgotten, and seemed never to know, not once, how to speak.

Almost everything was cleaned up or taken, or thrown away. There was only what he hadn't known. He lifted the manhole cover to the space between the ceiling and the slant of the roof. The flooring was covered in flat, schoolbook-type diaries.

His mother, nameless woman, had been the mistress of eduard roschmann, an *s.s. obersturmführer*, dubbed the *Butcher of Riga*, and she recorded EVERYTHING he did to her, and EVERYTHING she witnessed. The terror. The humiliation. The almost elegant lies and *wagneresque* style.

No one knew of her, or of the father of the child she carried, once she finally escaped, and eventually landed — a refugee from a futile Europe — in Australia. Not one person, living, in her lifetime, knew what she knew. Her son did not know who his mother really was. He'd never thought of her as young. Or beautiful. Violated, molested, tortured, horrified. She'd just baked, disappeared, died. So...

I know how it's been, or is, for most of you. Wildlings in boxes called

apartments, or houses, or flats. Upright, windowed coffins for us privileged, while some, on the streets, ask where their next fix is coming from, or *where'd y'score the tent, mate?* People being weird... I mean, fearful or lovely, when for most of your life they've been strangers who've ignored you. The confusing maelstrom of social media and selfie celebrity status. But I guess, just for a moment, all that exhaust, and all those big-mouthed bullies telling you what to eat and how to look better than your beautiful born bodies already are, shuddering in their rhinestones, their filler needles looking somehow redundant, have gone as quiet as the dead woman.

Furry bits finally, or momentarily, get their liberation and reprieve from the wax or the razor.

Yes, we've known this was coming. Me, and tarot, that scammy bastard that throws up the *devil card* like a random fungal thing between summer toes, where sand and sunshine should be. And yes, I've got the car trunk packed and a chainsaw beside the bed for the next desperate addict who decides to try breaking in.

However—

Stay the course, Critters. Keep that wildness keen. Hone it. Train. Be as real as you've always told me you are. Cook and plant, stitch and draw, write by hand in some forlorn and abandoned *to-do* diary. Because *to-do* is today. Be covert cabals of magic and wisdom.

I want to explain to you what I know is happening but to do so is a really long rant but... again... this was all predicted. This glitch. This is destiny. I haven't got to Reykjavík yet, but I probably will, if that helps hearten the confused among you. I'm exhausted. I'm running with color and considered rebellion, all the more to make it really ready for you because it's you, travelers who've sat with cards in hand— the weird, the pierced, the inked, the porcelain, the polyamorous, the artistes of flesh and song, the travelers of abused and forgotten places, the lawyers defending the rights of brumby, greyhound and thoroughbred, christmas puppies for the needle.

The Trans, the Thief, the Mother and the Battered have inspired me with every, every story you have shared, or that we have exposed. You are all so courageous and so fucking gritty!

We've been groomed, Wildlings, into submission. How about that?

Look in more directions than left or right, because they are not changing. Only in and out and down are doorways now.

Your eyes-wide-open is what is required of you. And me. And the person, whose name I never knew and was never destined to know anyway.

What are we to make of all this, hmm? Something rare, dear darlings.

Something of a treasure of tales, and a raven-chair of storytellings. I know you have, hidden, that which you dare not say aloud. So here is a moment...

Write. It. Down. Who you are. What you dared tell no one. Then hide it. Let tomorrow's child find it and wonder who the fuck you really were.

...

CHANGELING

Who am I kidding?

Mother is from another world. Some mythic *bansídhe* who left her magical child in one of the cradles in a ward of nameless, identical cradles, in a catholic arena of *nundom*: an abundance of rejected newborn people-puppies. Those of mortal women.

In legend, she does that. Occasionally. Abducts a human infant and endows them with gemstones and a temporary illusion of regency. Deep down within the citadels of the hollow hills of faerie she glamors herself and seduces some king of the *gypsies* into a night's wild sex on a midsummer's eve; of incalculably intoxicating revelry. I know.

She couldn't give a brass penny, as the *gentry* are known to not, but he's been hunting for me ever since. For years, while sitting in a café, sipping lattes and reading Charles de Lint, in the warm, tropical late spring sunshine, I anticipated the arrival of brothers. He would send them first, you must understand, because I could bolt at the sight of the splendor of this father. Him. His height. His bear-ness. His untamedness. His lustrous hair and moustache; eyes alight with wit and the wisdom of a horse whisperer. His *majesty*.

These oddly-dark-eyed and hazel-dappled, mismatched wild boys, three of them, always three of them, will turn every enchanted head as they stride to the table at which I lounge and, in voices rich with the Highland narrative of bog, peat, heather, *laphroag* single malt whisky off an Hebridean islay and, of course, the dusky, wet smell of cattle, the ginger-haired brother tells me it is time to come home. I have duties now that I am of an age. Mother has changed her callous, indifferent mind and wishes me to take her place because she fancies becoming mist and snow and ice and mountain lake, for

an eon or two, in what is now known as Newfoundland. I have storms to invoke
and ancient texts to plant for the future archaeologists to find, and consider factual by some agreed-to speculation, about a long disappeared race of seeming *giants*, or *kelpies*, or *Gentle Annis* of the Wild Hunt legend, because everyone knows time does not exist and that events do not progress in a straight line... after all, who is right? And is any of anything real anyway or was the *Truman Show* the most astonishing art to ever terrify?

The part-mortal children I bore will be fine. I have taught them well how to live amongst the human species. They have all been on stage. One has given a bloke, playing a *jesus*, a bloody good whippin while the other, in braids and ex-army cammos, has shone—reveled—as Eddy, for our down-home version of *Rocky Horror*. Daughter—a girl/woman—was *Juliet* in one story, *Columbia* in another, director, car-bonnet diver, photographer; the kid who, when first entering high school, informs the religious instruction teacher that she is the *devil's* daughter when asked why she chooses to dress in black clothing. A youngster who was to take to detention (the quiet room) as though it was Balmoral castle.

I don't even know what begins the hunt. I'd been told of this mythic flesh-and-blood mama when I was twenty two years old. I had a living child who might inherit something nasty. I should know of the sparse specter of a somewhat mediocre and fleeting event that birth is.

I am informed, after the interminable spectacle of this pacing, hand-wringing, mortified woman, that I knew was not a mother, that I'd always known was a *pretender*, weeping out *oh-my-dear-god/s* for over an hour, "Oh, dear god! Now listen, or else! We chose you; you were wanted. You were special. We paid £300 for you. Don't tell your sister, I don't want her to hate me. We saved you from an orphanage. Please don't look for her while I'm alive. It'd kill me.

Please make me a cup of tea and get me a *Vincents Powder*, I feel sick."

And that's the end of that. Life goes on. This story is not about what else I did or have done or will do. No. This story is concerned with honesty, not somebody's *idea* of truth, when that's a delusion of the worst kind because there cannot possibly be such a thing.

There's is only the opinion, of an arrogant species puffed up with its theory that it was made in the image of the PR'd-out-of-all proportion-ungod. Nothing about the violence of reality is necessarily anything more than the posturing of some incidental animal that breeds *way* too much, and thinks itself way too significant when, after all, those 600 million, million hemoglobin cells have as much right to name their successors as we do cats.

...

THAT OTHER WITCHCRAFT

Everything has consequence.

WITCHCRAFT AGAIN

Witchcraft is not a practice. Does it involve ceremony? Yes. We are discussing *draíochta*, after all. The awareness that if you or I have a geis that intimates that, if we even light a candle when there's no blackout, we're on the lam. Yet, it's okay to smoke a stranger's body, with smoldering branches and fronds of ogham, as they walk into the experience of ancestral healing, called *Rivers in the Skin*. There is nothing generic about the individuality of witchery. Once we know the river, and the valley, maelstrom has spoken our names...

If you and I relate to being custodians of wisdom, who understand *draíochta*, what does that mean? It means they will know us. In jeans and a faded out old Guns n Roses T-shirt, feet calloused from walking the dirt road barefoot, hands carrying a ratty old pack of tarot cards from one town to the next. They will know us.

THEY WILL KNOW US

We carry ancestral lands woven into skin and wit. Wolf-mother solidarity with arctic furriness. Pinion-feather landing at their feet, at the shrine to some bullshit god or other, just as they decide to walk away. You pick me up, by your trust, and I do so for you. We haunt the memory of unnamed mothers with an attitude of graceless snobbery, and we are always lost. We are never owned but I, and likely you, have been, and we therefore disagree with how to behave. Humbled by the smallest of rock formations that tell of ice ages, once experienced, while some of us bleach and wither under a blazing *otherland* sun.

We recognize kindred and ancestral craft in the Dublin museum. We pass our other selves on Jackson Avenue, downtown Queens, in New York, and raise both hands in the applause of deafness, to Zoey Salucci-McDermott, the *fuck-you*, Cobargo firefighter who refused to shake Morrison's hand. We are the ballot box absolving those who thought they voted, but were conned last time, who got it right this time through sheer force of will. A cup o' strong coffee and the heartbeat beneath the rubble in Beirut.

We are *Leòdhais*, in the Outer Hebrides, and *Ellan Vannin*, ghosts of Ynys Môn's forest that Paulinus burned out of spite. The Eden river, raging west to nor'east, that a king named *james*, thought was as close to *paradise* as any man could imagine. The intentional slow, traumatic drowning of sharks, for fin soup, *yves st laurent*, wrinkles and attitude. The mourners of Freddy Mercury and elizabeth 2, both queens of a sort. Although, really, Freddy *does* take the crown.

We are Amhairghin Glúngheal and the song of the *stag of many tines*, the *strange fruit* of Marion, Ophelia's iron vest on *Desolation Row*, the camels of the Ghan and Muruoa atoll, before, and after, the bombs.

The midnight hour is when words tumble, blackwater plummets through the cleft of weathered limestone on the way to the sea of Dover, from some secret infancy sometime during the Silurian epoch, and when the human being, who wears you or I as one body or another, removes their impotent humanity from the possibilities of magic's intimacy. Witching hour is the denial of an hour as a pretense of forever. Sunrise on the Negev, an icebound, winter killing season in Prague, first frost psilocybin and your nightmare of Kristallnacht. The drowning of a slave ship and the rotting dead of the *Ryme of the Ancient Mariner*.

    NO GODS

No gods, but with maps and chariots, over stony ground; with starlight to guide us and the songs and stories of forever (it sometimes seems) and nothing forgotten. No gods but each other, and the endlessness

of that. No gods but the awaited completion of an unfinished story.

We are *that other witchcraft*, and no book will ever tell anyone what that is. One can try—I sure have—but, as is the way of trying, it is inherently flawed. Too many stars to count and too many revolutions to recognize.

We are not the ones *alex sanders or margot adler* ever knew. We are the children of the ones the church didn't drown. The ones your mothers couldn't abort and the ones from an infinitely unrealized tomorrow. And yes, we talk with trees and snowmelt and the doorframes of possible future houses. Because you know the legend of the stander in the doorway, don't you?

Do I know who I am? Most certainly. Is that honest? Yes.

...

OF MICE, MARTIAL ARTS AND A VAGINAS

I once pushed three living human babies from this body. Doing so is outrageous, dangerous and really, quite seemingly, both impossible and ridiculous. It's a grunting, sweating, death's-head-grimacing surprise. That pain. Like a large brick object, with long, impossible fingernails seeking purchase in the muck of mucous and blood that also leaks from me without consent. Wise in the primordial ways of peristalsis, the unborn grinds, inexorably, along a narrow, but infinitely expanding *passage-to-air-from-water-disney-ride* that is a vagina.

Amazing things, vaginas.

To think I once thought this orifice was a tidbit, attached as an afterthought to a clitoris and other fleshly exuberances, thought of, in the beginning of time, by some benevolent mystical femme deity, for the sole purpose of self-gratification.

AFTERBIRTH

I suckled these people who had been expelled from this flesh and blood body. Examined their poo, before cleaning it from their skin with scientific precision. I experienced an absurd pleasure—a sense of being righteous—as each of them burped without vomiting on me. I never slept. I have known love.

Next, the terror. Two, three months into their tiny lives. Me waking to daylight. Why have they not screamed for me to do their bidding two hours before sunrise, as usual? How did I sleep through what is sure to be a living nightmare? By all that's worthy of praise, have I slumbered through their death? I race to their room to find them smearing the wall, artfully, intentionally and creatively. Intently and silently. With their own excrement.

Losing them to school. Do I know the cage into which I have thrust them? Uniformed, peer-pressured, comparing and comparative? In the hope they will achieve seeming-success under a captor's *terms-and-conditions*-layer of well thought out concrete that will pull them to the bottom of the bay as surely as the Titanic on an arctic night? Destined for conformity and questionlessness? Into an idealized but bullshit existence, selling insurance, becoming a doctor or a lawyer (forgive me, *mother mary*, I didn't know how glaring delusions actually can be until I reached, oh, forty five). The right to a mortgage and an upgraded car. And a cat. And an opinion accompanied by a *you're SUCH a control freak* comeback by your teenager. And botox. And redundancy. Oh, and a corona virus or some such, later: an interesting pathogen that mutates and causes the bubonic plague to seem edible.

To push them away. To hold them too close. To teach them to be safe. This is parenthood. This is incalculable anxt. No, it's okay. I kept them safe. They're alive—and adults now. Aren't they? Didn't I?

    TO BE SAFE

What a liar. How have I taught safety?

I did not take them to Ethiopia during the famine and made sure they helped carry the babies to the UNHCR tents. I did not drag them to Utopia to have them comprehend what growing up without garbage collection is like, now the people there have been taught (by the same system that has schooled these children) to be unlearned: of the wisdom of hunting, and seasons, and playing in a river. I have not grabbed them, now, and caught a flight to Lebanon to help erect shelter after the brutality of the blast. And, no matter how I cajoled, I did not keep them away from sugar. I talked. The thing we do when we can't do anything else.

CHILD KILLER

This is not self-abnegation—I have long ago sliced the smug and condescending smile from guilt's perennial face. It is realization. I did not teach them. Nothing. I have thought long and hard about this. I caved, is what I did. I thought of them as 'mine' when that is clearly a shocking arrogance. I *did* keep them from predators, though, didn't I? No, I did not. I let them drink coca cola. I allowed them birthday cakes. I didn't wonder at the additives or the artificial coloring. At the madness of balloons in the intestines of pelicans. I doomed them to indoctrination.

To reliance.

Even though all three of them—today—are living bodies, what of lore?

VIOLENCE

I am talking about the presumption of many that it's okay to be cruel. That to have a dwelling in which to stay dry, a body has to go into debt to complete strangers. In the current era, to be successful, it's necessary to drink alcohol to be thought sophisticated, even though it's a toxin. To wear four inch stilettos and get a conceptually-long labia sliced to an appropriately fashionable size, to sift through several thousand images of ourselves to find *the one* that sends the message: *feisty but available*, on the tinder app.

I am also talking about the presumption that World War 3 will not decimate Melbourne, or Sydney, or London, or Beirut tonight, while we sleep. The forgetfulness of all the women from Boudega to Emily Wilding Davidson, Wounded Knee, the Tasmanian Black War, Bergen-Belsen, the Clearances, the Slave Trade, David Dungay Jnr, Bobby Sands, Stonewall and the right to beat one's children to within an inch of their lives, and to buy one or two if the church has an abundance, from shamed women who should have known better than to dress for rape, even though they were never told about rape. The abduction, of non-Anglo-European, animist, healthy and ancestrally-taught hunter/gatherer children, institutionalized—safe—behind razor-wired protection facilities. The burning-for-profit of primordial Forests and bugger all the animal-people who live there. It's lumber, that's the word I was looking for. Not trees, no, that hints at sentience and we can't have vivisection if we agree to sentience. The disposable face masks and disease-laden, unincinerated latex gloves, the feeding frenzy of a corporate cocaine snack, food freedom destined to induce obesity and type 2 diabetes before the age of twelve, and the ideology of religion, blatant or obtuse, dooming offspring to a life of privilege or paucity.

Violence is not always a broken face or an amputated limb. Violence is also given kindly: ice cream, pizza, chips, beer, champaign, advice.

MIRROR, MIRROR

This is not about what we can't change. Like the plastic in your house, your office, your car. The glare of primary colors, neon, ruined music, and the hallucinatory, unspeakably mindless volume of non-essential products in a supermarket or online, a person's capacity to believe in advertising balderdash, and to trash Manila for the cost of an upgraded iphone.

No, this is about fear.

I never taught the children whom I birthed what to fear. I never knew they needed to know that.

FEAR

Have you watched a mouse being chased by a cat? They are remarkable! And most of the time they get away. Why? Because they are afraid. They don't want to be eaten. Deep in Mouse-person's ancestral brain is the DNA-memory of being consumed whilst still alive, awake and capable of knowing that their left leg is now missing. What's astonishing, is that even while being in the same situation—for THE FIRST TIME—mouse-person knows the way this could go. So, they run. An understatement, don't you agree? They DON'T JUST RUN! They weave and dart, use shadow like Johanne Sebastian Bach composing the *Brandenburg concerto*... good goblins-and-garden-gnomes, they fucking-well FLY when they leap between the adjacent building's highest wall and the compost heap far below.

All because their body-memory, womb to womb, vagina to vagina, taught them to be afraid. Is that why human babies cry, with such desperation and denial, when they first breathe air? Because they are afraid? They ARE afraid. And the first thing us larger mammals do is assure them, with a coo and a pat, that everything is alright. They are safe. Look, here's the nipple, now suck on this.

That's okay. But there comes a time. I don't know. Is it at a year old? Three? Seven is way too late. But then, twelve? Having lived into the double digit years, and never being chased by a great white shark whilst paddling at Balmoral beach, doesn't make a person safe. Having fed them *kinder surprise* after the tanty in the supermarket is not a protection, nor is it an immunity booster. Swimming lessons are excellent but, knowing what's underneath them in deep water is not usually part of the curriculum.

In the classic *Dune* series, Frank Herbert invents the *Bene Gesserit* (I know, I emoted almost exclusively to them in late teens), one of whom—the *Reverend Mother*—dares *Paul*, the future *Mau'dib*, to place a hand in a box whose contents are unknown. Apparently, he'll die if he doesn't, and could quite likely die if he does. He puts his hand in the box. Then comes the bullshit. Probably the only bullshit in the entire series (of which I am still enamored). A litany embraced by other idiots (I believed it once), like the unequivocal need for a hot shower in the morning:

> *I must not fear. Fear is the mind-killer. Fear is the little-death that brings total obliteration. I will face my fear. I will permit it to pass over me and through me. And when it has gone past I will turn the inner eye to see its path. Where the fear has gone there will be nothing. Only I will remain.*

And what a load of utter puerile nonsense is THAT?

Mouse would never get away from Cat. Woman will continue to be beaten, those people called *homeless* will continue to be viewed by a suited, and indebted-to-the-hilt population, as somehow lacking, when, in actuality, they are tribal.

Fear *hones* us. It gives us an edge—enough—to whisper *who can help me*? And to sometimes—*sometimes*—get an answer.

Fear is going to happen to you. Has happened. Is happening. If you and I are not provided a level of insight regarding this protection we, or those we love, will be hurt because, trust me, *not one* inhabitant of the Warsaw ghettos said to themselves or their families, *Oh yes, cattle trucks, what a good idea. Grossaktion Warsaw, hmm. Sure. It seems like a good premise to pack, don't you agree?*

NO ONE DOES ANYTHING

Martin Gilbert [3] writes: *In every ghetto, in every deportation train, in every labor camp, even in the death camps, the will to resist was strong, and took many forms. Fighting with the few weapons that would be found, individual acts of defiance and protest, the courage of obtaining food and water under the threat of death, the superiority of refusing to allow the Germans their final wish to gloat over panic and despair.*

No. We are fed the propaganda that the people just went.

---

[3] *The Holocaust: The Jewish Tragedy*, Sir Martin Gilbert, 2021

And here, in what's left of Gondwana:

> *Generations of Australians have been taught that no wars have ever been fought on Australian soil. Yet as many as 20,000 black Australians died fighting a war of resistance that lasted for more than a century* [4].

Bussamarai,

Calyute

Dhakiyarr Wirrpanda,

Dundalli,

Pemulwuy

When I was a kid at school I was never taught their names. Propaganda says they didn't mind us coming here, infecting their blankets, giving them grog and taking their children. Oh, let's build a bronze statue and erect it where our ancestors are now grass. C'mon. It'll be fun! Like playing Rio Tinto in the caves of the Pilbara!

They were afraid.

And that fear made them strong. Much as the colonialist regimes would have us believe to the contrary, the many First Nation's offspring are still here.

Fear is *not* the enemy. Fear is the immediately necessary story, told to Mouse, by their own body. It says: *you are under attack*!!!! Fear permits us to release massive floods of proactive force into our bloodstream. Fear fuels us to run, to scream, to resist.

Necessary for us to defend. To be brave. It is the event: the terrifying, immanence of violation and destruction that releases this

---

[4] *Six Australian Battlefields*, Marji Hill & Al Grasby, 1998

ancient, ancestral juice of visceral, overwhelming brilliance and audacity—the *response* to threat—that we must work at paying attention to. That we must teach our children to recognize. To know how to not freeze (the third, and most unsatisfactory, of the *f* words here: *fight, flee, freeze*).

WHY WE TRAIN

I've been quiet as to why, over the many decades, I have learned several martial arts. Why I have done this physicality. Hapkido, aikido, MMA, iaido. Free weights, until I have shoulders that look like small, striated melons allowing me to be capable of lifting the front end of a bubble car from where it was seemingly, irrevocably bogged. I don't have to provide a reason, do I? Was there one? Absolutely. Did I save the kids I raised from harm? Just. Did violence occur more than once? In so many ways that I refuse to talk about it.

I trained hard. Because I knew fear. Then, as I grew older and became "unfuckable" I almost thought about stopping. But no. Because some instinct didn't want me balancing dissolving bones in a steel walking frame at aged 60. Because I'd thought I was safe enough to be lazy; wizened enough to get away with eating jelly? Perhaps.

Then came the phone call. A couple of nights ago. From a friend, decades younger than me and in actual danger, albeit not from someone in her house, but from a predator who was coming for her. She, too, had pushed a human being from her vagina. The experience of that is one thing, the threat implied from a man who considers himself privileged—who WANTS her, despite her—has her caged and in hiding. Terrified. Not knowing what to do if he comes to her door, no matter how clever she's been at avoiding him. So far.

And here it is. I show her. Old woman things. Bokken. Bow. How to throw a punch. How to cripple a leg. How to grab him in a clutch and drive a knee over and over and over, into his kidneys. To know how strong she truly is.

How unexpectedly accurate a strike with a jo staff can be; how absolute the concussion. To know the ramifications of self-defense under the law (not too jolly). What to expect if she actually kills him. If that is the only option because the cops place an *apprehended violence order* (AVO) on him and he comes around the following night, in the silence of 4 a.m., and sets fire to her house.

To be so utterly confident that she might—just might—react with the ferocity of that mouse, if the situation becomes necessary.

TEACH THE FUTURE

Teach your kids what fear feels like. Let them understand that their bodies produce the antidote to predation. Don't sit them down and suggest—after a small, uncontrollably vicious dog has bitten their arm and made it bleed—that they relax and breathe deeply. Get them to say to a pillow *I do not mean you harm, but we must kill the monster together. And you need, now, like me, to learn to be as ready to live as the wiliest-ever mouse that EVER was,* and then have said child beat the pillow on the bed, over and over and over, until they are lathered in sweat, have cried and cried at how far their trust of dogs has retreated from their capacity for trust... until they are done. Until the cortisol has left their bloodstream and they can heal.

An animal's (human or otherwise) stress-response system is usually self-limiting. Once a perceived threat has passed, hormones return to normal. As adrenaline and cortisol levels drop, heart rate and blood pressure return to baseline normalcy, and other systems resume their relentless living activities. But when stressors are always present and a person feels constantly under attack, hyper-vigilance is the result. We stays turned on. The long-term activation of stress-response, and the overexposure to adrenalin, cortisol and other danger-induced hormones can disrupt almost all our animal-body processes. This puts us at increased risk of many health problems, including:

- *Anxiety*
- *Depression*
- *Digestive problems*
- *Headaches*
- *Heart disease*
- *Sleep problems*
- *Weight gain*
- *Memory and concentration impairment*

That's why it's so important to learn healthy ways to navigate life's stressors.[5] Soft, gentle words can come later. Any time. All the time. That's also just wonderful. But not at the expense of our children's lives, their sanity, their self-worth or their relationships, when *you* are no longer able to provide them with the truth of the world. Or worse. If you knew the truth of the world and you have told them they were safe, despite it. Told them that you will always keep them safe, when that is a lie.

You can't. You won't. You didn't. You wish somebody had had this conversation with you. You need your own crash pillow that has agreed with the process. You need to teach the child—and know it for yourself—that mice are ferocious when the need arises, and there is the possibility of escape. You need to open the cage door.

Fear is not the enemy. An enemy is the enemy. Fear can save your life.

---

[5] https://www.mayoclinic.org/healthy-lifestyle/stress-management/in-depth/stress/art-20046037#:~:text=Cortisol%2C%20the%20primary%20stress%20hormone,fight%2Dor%2Dflight%20situation

...

WOLVES IN CAGES

Confused, isolated, anxious and seemingly dislocated? Insight can seem impossible when we don't see ourselves reflected in media, either social or advertised. Suggestion? Include *yourself* in the narratives. In the myths. In the legends. As one character or another.

Who you genuinely love, and who you really are. In wild, blackberry-bramble and bird's nest weavings that can help you recognize the traumas of initiation that may have trapped you within the man-made metal teeth of strangers.

Be easy on yourself. You are all there is, in this.

...

BRAVE

I am stronger than fear

—Malala Yousafza

SORRY TALK

Australia, 2013, prime minister Julia Gillard, makes a bold statement. In a televised conference, before the entire nation, she apologizes for the forced adoptions that have been perpetrated in this country. This apology, while significant, is typical of politics insofar as those of us born of a concept of enforced stigma and shame are not addressed down in the basement of honesty. I wept along with all those people in the packed auditorium, whilst internally seething, thinking *what of us?*

What. Of. Us?

It is not enough to take into account the many, and harrowing, statements of women abandoned, disrespected, snubbed and bullied by child-thieves. Those of us—our heritage, ancestry, unbroken belonging—misappropriated through expediency and out of the bureaucratic conscience of public pressure, have not had our say. At least I haven't.

STATEMENT OF SURVIVAL

I was purchased as entertainment of for older kid who needed distracting. The effect of this nearly killed me when, eventually, I had had enough of 'go fetch'. It certainly instigated an unhealthy fear of, and cobra-like attraction to, the idea of love, if not love itself (a word

I find quite underwhelming in its genericism). An obsession to belonging that I doubt can be overcome.

Why were the offspring of these disregarded and degraded women and girls not seriously addressed in that apology? Because the consequences and the depths of iniquity were not only underrepresented in the report, our existence, as people *apart* from the mainstream of society, have not been given a language.

I was bought. An *Eeyore* with, sooner rather than later, a belligerent and defiant attitude. I was struck if I displayed autonomy and independence of spirit. I was punished severely for intelligence, usually by weeks of being ignored. That was before the owners learned the drugging trick. But I was, from as young as I remember, never provided with instruction. What were the rules?

Somebody, *please* explain the fucken rules.

I am *woman*. A female mammal. Mother. Definitely. Androgynous, certainly. What is that? A person who carries a living infant in a uterus. With a body that summons testosterone, like a queen summoning a gilded carriage or Arnie winning some *mr. universe* title. I am as thrilled to be intertwined with as concrete an ability to conceive, and propel living people into the world, as I am at pumping iron and wielding daisho in a dojo. And that's this body, not my *ness*. You have to be brave to display your *ness*, at any time, if that *ness* is divergent.

BOXES

As at birth, so now, at almost seventy years living, I recognize boxes are powerful things. Some imply choice – a clever trick, almost, but not quite liberating. A tick in a particular box, invented by clerks at the behest of their employers'/government's/religious insistence, will categorize you, stamp you with a presumed identity. Similar to the demand of government, or the abbot of some medieval copyist monastery demanding the *Leabhar Gabhála na hÉireann* include some nonsensical reference to the "sons of Noah". What do those boxes make anyone? How do they interpret an individuality? Can they? On paper, yes. Because... and here's the point: we are *made*. But no. We have a voice. We can challenge coercion. We can demand the boxes vanish.

Upon the discharge of the erroneously titled *adoption*, on December 1st, 2020, in a *supreme court*, I had Eduard Jean Manso de Villa's name written, officially, on a renewed birth certificate. It was his sperm impregnated the woman who bore me. Is that important? I didn't know who he was until a year prior. Yes, significant.

I am, however, still waiting for a rule book.

> FOR THE TERM OF THEIR NATURAL LIFE

> *Refusal to participate is a moral choice. Water is a gift for all, not meant to be bought and sold. Don't buy it. When food has been wrenched from the earth, depleting the soil and poisoning our relatives in the name of higher yields, don't buy it.*

> —Robin Wall Kimmerer, *Braiding Sweetgrass*

> TRUTH

Truth is, I've been lying most of this life. I remember when I *knew* I was doing it, but I didn't know the rest of the time. It was just a way of being. Of attending to the name and the circumstances that I'd somehow, sometime, been convinced into assuming was the real me. The person born, registered, authorized and identified, by everyone else, *except* me, *as* me.

There's this odd saying going around, here in the so-called *western world*—among many people in what's titled an alternative movement—an expression that doesn't make any more sense than religion, or hunting other animals to extinction or the news, or what keeps us healthy. Truth. I've had people want to disagree with me over the most ridiculous things like whether vegetarianism is healthier for us creatures to eat than the flesh of other animals. When I inevitably question the validity of their unresearched conclusions they, invariably, tell me, close up, *well, that's your truth...* as though there was an Ikea of *truthdom*; as though there is a choice and as though anything is known, ever, if we're honest. Because honesty isn't the same thing as truth, and I don't figure there's ever been such a thing as truth. I wonder who made the concept up?

Truth is not the same critter as fact, either. There's truth and then there's *a* truth, or even *your* truth, but when these terminologies enter a conversation there's always something of the righteous about the attitude of the person proclaiming the accusation of difference in their sentence. They curl their lip, or observe their challenger of learned ideology, like the purveyor of *jehova's witnesscism*, as though you, we... I am a problem. As though they have some special secret, and that enough people are in this elite cabal for me not to be if I don't agree.

A saying exists, amongst christian folk, about some mythic dead bloke, whom the Greeks of the day named *jesus* (a *joshua*-type renaming). That he is the offspring of an omnipotent, singular, male, loving, jealous, and vengeful god, and that being slaughtered in such an horrific and blood-crazed way was going to save every human animal from the curse of Eve, forever. That he was going to die for us. For us. When he begged his daddy to stop the execution there was nada. Go ahead. This is the only way we're going to change society and get these willful, self-determined upstart-animals that Yaldabaoth concocted in his boredom, to abide by a set of MY rules, rules like *thou shalt not kill* without a clause that exempts war, genocide, ecocide and *honor killings*; rules that the cabal at Nicaea and Whitby and, oh, for generations of unborn little brides of christ, and handsome altar boys, will willingly break: the chastity rule, the rich man won't enter the kingdom of heaven rule... and whoever thought up poverty, obedience, humility and no sex... those nutters, in abominably unfashionable frocks, shaved bald patches, round or pointy hats and scarves (reads a bit like *scottish grandmother-wear*) who thought up a stone-rolling, rise-up on the third day of what should have been honest putrescence, resurrection zombie shit rule, and that the poor bastard-on-a-cross, dying slowly of an unthinkable torture because his papa went shtum when his adult son begged for a reprieve, is the *way, the truth and the life*, and I ask you: what does that mean? A bit like the threat of what would happen at an attempt at refusal of mandatory vaccinations, or the years in a detention center for escaping a brutal regime, perhaps. Being an *illegal* something.

If that ravaged, violated and decimated person, explicitly *that* violated person, did exist as a living, flesh-and-blood human being, he was killed, alongside every other seditionist, conscientious objector, farmer, weaver, healer, odd, indigenous, or enslaved person demanding a right to freedom, or any woman for any reason, anytime. *He* is the mythic *sacrifice* of the empire-of-the-day that will also cut down and burn any forest, poison any water source, in order to assuage a governmental need to maintain a warning or presume a right. *He* is the people protesting the invasion of their ancestral lands, by a regime that stole their homes, their means of perennial security, banned the culture, raped and enslaved women and girls, and boys (again) for that matter, and used their children, as they chose, when they weren't also shackled and sold off to salt mines or, later, cotton fields, rubber plantations or cattle ranches of, oh, I don't know, a hundred or two thousand acres of what had been indigenous territory.

Well, he rather overdid the project.

Because pf the above sounds an awful lot like the woman-killings of the *malleus malleficarum* years, the mass murder during the ergot outbreaks, the provision of smallpox-infected blankets and rum to the indigenous folk of every invaded country, waterboarding, impaling, gas chambering, Guantanamo Bay electrocution threatening and, here in what was once Gondwana, but that has been known as Australia since Matthew Flinders decided that southern land (terra australis) was too *nothing* a name for a continent that they had only just invaded and colonized, despite over five hundred indigenous kinship groups and an approximate million people already being here. Who, among us, really knows—or cares—about that? After all, invasion, slaughter, deaths both immediate and drawn out over centuries, are no longer problems, are they? Or are they? The shackling, hooding and humiliation, the cashless welfare card with all its pious implications, the deaths from suicide, kidney failure and incarceration of First Nation youth, remain commonplace (if sort of pretend-hidden) in the 2020s[i]. What of the breed-them-white policies? What of the residential schools and forced indoctrination into an authorized religion? Or an invented one, anyway?

A man-made threat. *Be careful, you will be cast out. Christ died for you, you willful, thankless and opinionated bastard!* Who are they now? How does a person come back from identity theft? Language theft? Non-uniformity and servitude? Do they? Can I?

JIGSAW PUZZLES

I was a liar for most of this life. Wasn't I? Or was it that I didn't tell the truth because I was told that the truth *was* the truth, and it wasn't? Not ever.

No one explained, you understand, that knowledge is a jigsaw puzzle.

For a lifetime I hadn't known what the end picture was supposed to be or, really, what the picture actually always was because it had been cut up into a myriad stack of tiny pieces, and some diligent squirrel-man had hidden away the corners, supposedly never to be found.

Was it even worth trying to figure out what color connected to what color; what pattern with what pattern? Especially me? Am I a color? Was I even in the picture or were the odd pieces scattered around the concrete dropped by mistake by captors? I couldn't even begin to understand the game because I didn't know what the reality was. I was afraid to ask. In case I was right. Because if I was right and life as I knew it was a lie then who was I? I didn't understand the rules.

Never understood the rules.

THROUGH THE LOOKING GLASS, OH ALICE

Sin began with a woman, and we must all die because of her (25:24)
—the book of ecclesiasticus (circa 175 BCE)

What happens to you when you think you know a right way to be; when the narrative you have been told that is the appropriate behavior for a girl, or a woman, is not who you are? Is not who I am, nor ever was? I have a distinct feeling that anyone reading this is, about now, contemplating whether I am drunk, mad, unstable, out of it on something very cocaine-*ish*, and rambling. I'm not.

I'm working the rope in and out of this perilous and potentially deadly and collapsible mineshaft – hauling this bucket of bullshit by this feeble, politically-engorged windlass so fucken hard that I've skun the knuckles on bloody fists; the life lines and the fate lines on the palms of my hands are now raw and burned from the weight and the rasp of the rope. These here shoulders are bruised and desiccated deep down within the muscle.

I'm mining for the words to attempt to understand, let alone express, what this is: this lie, so recently exposed and executed, of who I have lived as, and how I've lived; of why I write "what happens to a person" instead of being honest and saying "what happened to me..." Why I cringe a little at the implications of the word *my*.

IDENTITY

Is having identity important? To prove to the world that we have a right to be here? Yes. When it ain't had. And who is Eve if not *Havah*—life—and if that construct is mythically valid, then why is life considered as being an obstruction, in the way of something more important, when that phenomenon of importance is a lie? And, therefore, so also is the *sin of Eve* a crock-of-shit of a story.

Eve gets her name because the current trade language of the world is English, a fractured mosaic made up of the tapestry of conquerage. If I did not give this idea of *woman* an upper-case E, I could be talking of dusk, twilight, the last of the day before the darkness of night, and I'm not. Or am I? Why was she renamed Eve when she already had a name?

Who is she? And is she you? Is she me? Yes.

I'm writing about archetypal woman who, according to patrician logic, brought down the world, for goodness sake, presuming that the world, written of, was 'man'. That gave that dirty old misogynist, Augustine, a good excuse for *original sin*. As if World is not a multifaceted, intelligent individual who quite probably considers us inconsequential. Or worse, a meat to be mulched.

If I was a betting human (depending on one's interpretation of that term) I'd lay odds that the irony of the above is not lost on you, either. I might have been brought down by a lie, but I have never pretended.

FALLEN

> *This thought can turn us into bounty hunters for the acknowledgment we were denied. Some of us yell, some of us write screeds. These are ways of brute-forcing ourselves into the wrongdoer's mental space so they are compelled, at last, to think about us. Because as you say – nothing rankles quite like the thought of them blithely taking the last word to the grave.*
>
> —Eleanor Gordon-Smith,
> Thu 21 Jan 2021, *The Guardian News*

It is February. The dead zone. The darkest hours just before dawn. It's pissing down rain outside. I have stalked the lengths of a maze of hospital corridors since the day before yesterday and now, I am finally on my back. I have legs in stirrups and someone, masked and anonymous, is shoving several needle-piercings deep within the unseen area of my genitalia; unseen because this pregnant belly is enormous, and I haven't seen feet, let alone a pudendum, for weeks. I later learn that someone cut my perineum wide open to allow the body of the newborn human being to pass, more easily, from the cave of their nativity, into the world of *mankind*.

Some doctor at the maternity services section of the North Shore Hospital, I never find out a name, examined me, vaginally, when I was potentially three months pregnant, and took blood for pathological confirmation that I was *with child*; *up the duff*. He estimated a due date for birth, based on the speculative memory of an addled young thing's last menstrual period and, because I remained, in the moments prior to delivery, an individual person two weeks beyond that official date, I was both deviant and defiant, somehow. How dare I?

I am admitted to hospital, labor is induced, and I am given an enema just in case I shit when I push. Nothing a nurse should ever have to face the cleaning up of. We are supposed to do this quietly and cleanly, I am informed.

I pace, continuously, for sixteen hours. Why? If I sit down, the contractions stop. Owner-woman pops in occasionally, curious about a labor/birth experience she has never understood, excited in a way that I would, in coming years, learn was a narcissistic greed for possession of what or who I carry inside me. An impossibility for her. Why then, do I feel no compassion?

A nurse suggests this walking marathon. I don't know what to do, of course, so I follow orders. There has been no learning to breathe, garnering of information or experiment, in trial runs, with a birth-partner. Not then. Not if one is single, despite all staff calling me *you there*. Despite the liberation of our gender, or so it seemed on the surface of society, when nothing was further from reality.

I have been alive, as I understand that, for 19 years. Existence has changed for the better, both since leaving the psychiatric facility where I'd landed for giving up. For being tired of being afraid. A puppy supposed to be seen and not heard, with a political and spiritual opinion at variance to snob suburbia. I had (if one can *have* a disorder... is that like having a cold?) someone, unknown, tick a box, made up some shit called a *hysterical personality disorder*). Had I dropped LSD? Of course. Had I read Lobsang Rampa, Carlos Castaneda and Eric von Däniken? Yes. Was I aware of any deception? No. I really couldn't have given a fuck if there was. Blavatsky and Crowley? Yes. This is a new era. The dawning of the Age of Aquarius. The Peace Train. Flower Power after the terror of the nuclear bombs. Post-apocalyptic Auschwitz. Ann Frank. Acid Rain. The Beatles and Jimi Hendrix, Bob Dylan and Buffy Saint Marie. Odetta. Bury My Heart at Wounded Knee and Charlie Perkins. Martin Luther King still warm-souled, even as he is lowered into his grave.

I am looked at askance by most people because I am considered *strange*. I am young. I wear black, shave hair down to the follicles, refuse bras and dangle with ostentatious earrings. I have acne scars, line pale eyes with kohl. I am called a *beatnik* by quick-judging older people, prance a lot in seeming self-certainty, write poetry, busk on

Circular Quay, identify as witch or druid, because it is close... merely close, to what I would realize in later decades. I am deeply enmeshed in seances, writing, the seducing and shagging of boy-men, and the friendships of lesbians and radical academics. I drink, on a Saturday, with the motley crew at the Royal George Hotel and have a secret crush on both Bette Midler, and the guy behind the bar whose name I never discover.

I am street-savvy about some things, alone, except for the woman who owns me, and a turntable of hospital-approved midwives.
GIVE IT UP

That unnamed doctor is wrong. At four in the morning, I give birth to a living baby being. Twenty two hours into the trauma, invisibility and sterility of an unmarried woman's labor. I should be ashamed but I'm not. I'm nearly dead but look! This wee child's weight is 2.6 kilos, they have a thin sheen of white-blonde hair and, as I am to be educated to understand, they appear (as all newborns do) like an old, old, old person. He is taken from me immediately after the umbilicus is cut and I don't see him again until sometime after daylight. This tiny, shriveled, squinty, pale kid enchants me. Love, I guess. Who knows what love is?

Then the first of the social workers comes. That day, and every day thereafter, I am besieged by the beige neatness, and judgmentally pursed lips, and tilted head, of these government and church-sanctioned, clipboard-wielding be-hatted, be-gloved, invariably thirty-five year old women on a mission. The litany drones thus:

> *You can't keep it, you realize. Not without a husband.*
> *Give it to us. We can give it the family it deserves.*
> *What will people think? Being a bastard?*
> *What will it think when it goes to school, knowing its mother is a (insert insult)?*
> *You are dooming it to a lifetime of neglect. Here, sign the release form.*

You're a terrible young woman, you're being terribly, terribly selfish.
No man will ever want you.
You'll never find a man.
No man wants another man's castoff.
How will you support it?
Give it up.
You know how this will end, don't you?
You'll be on the streets with it. Is that what you want?
For the love of god, give it up.
The child needs two parents. Give it a chance at a normal life.
It needs two parents.
What can you give it?
You're a terrible...
How do you imagine you can raise it alone?
You'll never get a man.
No man will want it.
Give it up.
No man will ever want you.

Give it up.

Give what up? Are they talking about a living human child? This child at my breast?

I am allowed home after the stitches holding perineum skin to perineum skin are gouged out by what feels like a mattock or a spoon.

WHAT MOTHERS SAY

> *No nuns broke into our homes to kidnap our children. We gave them up to what we convinced ourselves was the nuns' care. We gave them up maybe to spare them the savagery of gossip, the wink and the elbow language of delight in which the holier than thous were particularly fluent. We gave them up because of our perverse, in fact, morbid relationship with what is called respectability.*
>
> —Enda Kenny, The Journal. IE, 2017[ii]

And yet, like the individual I worked with at a conference on pitching a story, who had lived in Sarajevo when the bombs had gone off down the road from the café, I was compelled—not to run from, but towards—the threat of personal ambiguity.

Because it's invisibility, absence, utter superfluousness as an individual, the lack of being in the club of people-with-relatives, that terrified me. Being alive is the result of those same pressures of unviability that compelled a girl/woman to be rid of me. Because I was an abandoned person, and I knew it. Beyond the shadow of doubt that had always been the agenda that I ran from, like christians running from Aboriginals, Africans, Sami, North American, South American and Canadian *Indians*, peoples of the Caribbean, the Pacific Islands, Aotearoa, oh, I'm sorry to those of you I am forgetting to add, before they were baptized into acceptability, not including the thousands of useful children ripped from their home streets during the British Child Migrant Scheme. Aware that rejection has a smell that is only registered by the limbi brain, sensed but not known, but that incites abandonment or attack anyway.

NEURONS THAT FIRE TOGETHER

Some of this begs the question of what constitutes motherhood. And, despite all manner of objections and justifications, Dr. Paul Sunderland, addictions psychotherapist, consultant and trainer in his essay *Adoption and Addiction—Remembered Not Recalled*[iii], notes from *Lifeworks Lecture*, sums up thus:

The human brain starts working before it is fully built. Experience is the architect of the brain. Experience is the cue for connections and hook-ups of the billions of neurons formed before birth. In other words, neurons that fire together, wire together. If life begins with a trauma of separation and abandonment, that feels life-threatening, that is how the neurons will fire and wire. The human brain is a reflective organ, reflecting on past experiences, so it would be normal for abandonment issues to always be there in relationships.

For the adoptee there is real fear in relationships. There is a great desire or hunger to attach, causing you to sometimes behave against your best interests, but with the conflicting feelings that this is not safe. The feelings are held in the limbic

system which will always override the frontal cortex, but it is the thinking brain – the frontal cortex which takes people into therapy.

Mothering is the process of growing a human being in a uterus. Feeding the unborn everything we consume, from avocados to cigarette toxins, from the *Cat in the Hat* story to James Taylor's *Fire and Rain*, headphones attached to a distended abdomen, horrifyingly producing purplish stretchmarks by the day, something no one ever discusses. Not before the internet, and online tutorials, that is. Long before many of us had a chance. Ugly scars, we thought. Deeply traumatized by Bianca Jagger and her dodging of the illegitimacy bullet, in 1970 when, at four months pregnant she married Mick. *She* wouldn't have had stretchmarks. He wouldn't have wanted her if she'd had stretchmarks. Would he? Did she?

Mother-*ness* includes our prenatal environment and, equally as fraught with danger and trepidation, what we say and how we think. What we are coerced into believing and how perverse and endemic is the notion of shame. The problems compound when those of us, diving into our right to gender and economic equality with men in suits and ties, are surprised by the conception-consequence, despite the era being one of a newfound contraception revolution, the back street coat-hanger expert no longer required—well, not as often—and a biology that often overrides our sensibility.

Is mothering, per se, extended beyond pregnancy and birth? Can it be claimed by any woman? No. I contest that and am up for the post-modern fight. According to the online etymological dictionary:

> MOTHER *(n. 1) "Sense of "that which has given birth to anything" is from late Old English; as a familiar term of address to an elderly woman, especially of the lower class, by c. 1200.*

Of course, I am wary of many online opinions. Many, or most, speak from a bias of populist, dogmatic, social or algorithmic constructs. And I am averse to all because I have lived as a liar and agreed to the deceits presented to me as facts from as far into time as I am able to recall.

THE POINT

The point is, that awkward delve into who, or what, a person really is, that began after the death of the final living owner of this flesh and blood body in 2002; a black market thief who shall be nameless for the remainder of this story, because—well—bully for her and any sense that I might be civil in regards this matter. The deaths of this final captor finally meant the annulment of that promise. It resulted in meeting a once-imagined mother. I was given the only thing I could use: the name of the man who had inseminated her. For what remained of a harrowing and otherwise uneventful day, I heard nothing but her interest in her own life and achievements. No discussion of feelings, intimidation, intimacy with her lover—a father for me. Her time on the Yorkshire Moors as a child, one's place within any sort of family heritage; an utterly unilateral piecemeal rhetoric that had obviously been rehearsed. There it was: the narrative. An excuse. No discussion of women and shame and what might have become of me. Once or twice I tried to bridge the subject, but I sensed her... repulsion? Intimidation? Something in her eyes that wanted to keep the conversation to a script. I think it's called trauma, although she thought of it as shame.

SLAVERY AND THE SLEEPER

> *According to the Protocol to Prevent, Suppress and Punish Trafficking in Persons Especially Women and Children, trafficking in persons means the recruitment, transportation, transfer, harbouring or receipt of persons, by means of the threat or use of force or other forms of coercion for the purpose of exploitation. Exploitation includes prostitution of others or other forms of sexual exploitation, forced labour or services, slavery or practices similar to slavery, servitude or the removal of organs. The consent of the person trafficked for exploitation is irrelevant and If the trafficked person is a child, it is a crime even without the use of force.*
> —United Nations
> *International Day for the Abolition of Slavery*, Dec (1949)[iv]

ON THE OWNING OF A HUMAN ANIMAL

Entertainment for an older girl. No pay. It took me years to unravel what I had unwittingly accepted. An owner justified her story by enthusiastically explaining how the timing had been perfect. I was born on the eve of the solstice of December, the year after she had obtained the elder girl (I am unsure how). That meant I got to be a christmas present! Wasn't that perfect? They had the money, so... go!

How had it happened? How was it possible for an illiterate person (in difference to a non-literate individual who usually remembers heritage like legends, lore and ancestral kin) with an open cheque book, to buy a human that had just been born, just in time for the ho, ho, ho season? I mean, five days? Was it a whim? Did she wake up one day and think *oh! I know how to shut the little bastard up! I'll go to the nuns! I'll get her a sister. That should make her happy.* Because the sister-kid was not happy. She was sick. A lot. That made childhood tricky.

I was never provided with written instructions and had to make up the job description as the years unfolded. It is curiously vague. I was presented with certain things, like toys and books, so that sister-kid could take them. I had to hang around for whenever she misbehaved so that she could point the finger at me and suggest that I had done the theft, made the mess, left her cardigan at the bowling alley on her behalf, and on purpose. I had caused the woman to have to call the police when sister-kid vanished from the beach one summer evening, because I had not retrieved a towel from where she had left it. I had let her drown, hadn't I? The unwritten job description. I was a failure.

As the full impact of an impersonal curiosity began to grow roots in me, I begged life to stop talking. Look at what I had achieved? The task of being a scapegoat had become redundant now that the owner was dead. But no. I had not whistle-blown yet. The achievements are nothing when the roots that support the branches of *glitterdom* are shallow.

In 2003 I was at the beginning. I kept my head down. No one—not a best friend or any children—knew the sea into which I had just cast my ridiculously unprepared skiff.

LANGUAGE DEFINES A CULTURE

The point of an idea such as this, of dropping myself into this story, is that I reject the presumed necessity of writing in the parlance of academia. I have lived long enough in the shadow of bigotry and shame to come out the other side. What a betrayal of wisdom is the so-called authority that demands we shape the landscape-winding of language into the straightjacket-demanding, boot-crushing, chainsaw-revving of the forest voice, the throat song and mob-vocal indigenous clap stick, drum and stompfooted vowel and glottal-click, into the corset-and-whaleboned dialect of queen and state, rather than localized ancestral accent, the cane a bone-jarring slice across the palm, the hiss of an Anglo-righteousness murdering the dialect of moor and deep valley, that still hints at the conquerage of family, this Celtic/Gaelic and Breton tongue, overwritten by Rome, and its burr-like attachment to *latin* (canonical, medical, legal-speak, botanical, sublingual) including its offshoot of papish and military-political jargon, meant to affect us with a presumed authority.

STILL NO RULE BOOK

I write this (and no, I am not done yet) because it has taken me more than an average lifetime to
>a. comprehend that I am not dumb.
>b. realize I was not included in the senate report.
>c. approach the courts to gain legitimate freedom from captivity, also acknowledged as slavery.
>d. for offspring to understand me, themselves, their own children and their ancestral pride.
>e. because it has taken so long and
>f. perhaps, for anyone still living who is also confounded; who does not know what happened; who does not comprehend that they are not at fault for what they have been and, also perhaps, for what they have done.

I shall try resolving this by telling you, anyone still trapped by the boxes of shame, of thinking they had a choice and never did, just how brave you are to remain alive. To protect your shine. And if, like the people I mention on the acknowledgments page, you are a revolutionary, an activist, mad enough to help denude the atrocity of slavery and bias, well, you are simply almightily brave.

If nobody produces the rule book, appropriately and without connivance or agenda, then let it begin now, just in case any of us, still alive, who have already taken this Darkened Road, begin a fall from which we have no idea of recovery.

Just remembered, love. Take a light.

...

The Senate Inquiry into Forced Adoptions, Australia, 2010.
Australian Parliamentary Report on Child Migrants from the United Kingdom (online-only issue), 2010

Final Report of the Commission of Investigation Into Mother and Baby Homes, 2021

Adoption and Addiction, Dr Paul Sunderland, 2014

WON'T NEVER BE ME

ADDENDUM TO *BRAVE*

Won't it? Sure hope not. So, yep, travel the darkened road, love, but carry a light. Them mountains in the distance be you, forgotten. Them voices singin ancient lullabies, now, be you, too. Ridin on a wind that shrieks, threadbare, through weaving winding, rubble strewn alleys, through broken forests of dead hope. Now, laments of broken glass, discarded needles, a meth pipe and the bottom of a bottle at wine o'clock, rememberin when she promised, 'nah, it won't ever be me.'

'Crack it', the mountains say, 'this code of us. This face was never pretty, and our inheritance to you is in the shadow of every judgment without grace. Use it, the discernment. Just don't spread it too thin. No popes or unchanging governments gonna help you. Got no light, ya see? Just the mad poets and singers of songs and tellers of stories with a little deep to em. We got you.

No tables set with silverware, but these crusts are buttered. Necessary initiation, did we mention? Tippen yer hat to it, is to become a
grownup. Bring a bit of who you truly are to the feast. Oh, and honest lore? Where's the next true tongue comin from, and is the water of the river you drink from as clean as it seems?'

Travel the darkened road, you will, that's just a certain thing. But carry a light, love, cause there's others along the way, be dark, and take too much, eh? Be careful to know what you know, and not guess.

We told y'once, we tell yiz again, us mountains're tired of people gotta climb us to think emselves worthy.

...

KINGMAKER

A Letter to my Ancestral Father

Dear, dearest Father,

I'm alive. Still. I know we never met but here I am. Yes. I am here, and this time, in a body, I am woman. I have birthed the future over and over. And now I am wilderness. So, before I become the forest floor and a future generation of lichen and fungi to feed the dreamer, I figured it is time, now, finally, to say hello.

    I know you. You are a sleeper in the land of the immortal dead and yet I look at the back of my hand—at the wiry blood that sits just seconds beneath the skin of me—and there you are. A monarch in those valleys and mists and silent, deathly wet and callous white. Long at sea, I know how to sail. Long at war, I know how to fight. Big-talkin that allows me to slip through enemy thoughts and into the snow at the edge of time. Alone, but hey, you laid with someone, didn't you?

Father, life has been troubling. Without you to touch my hair, without you to fix my feet in shoes, of walrus hide that our mothers chewed before they taught you to sew, I am sunk deep in liminal sky twilight. Up to my chest. Up to my throat. In shallow, brackish talk and lore. You are not here to laugh when I am afraid. With the laugher that only a giant of a man can let loose. Laughter like the wind, wild amongst the harps that crest the hills to terrify an unknowing enemy. Laughter tinged with sadness, with no honest treaty for our grandfather oak—him, cut down and shredded to make the worthlessness of paper; and a promise never kept. Or else writ upon parchment, made from the skins of my tiny ungrown brothers, in difference to the stones that guide the navigator from Brignogan to Tŷ Mawr, and even further still, to the Stones of Stenness and the secret-exchanging, initiating inner earth chambers of Maeshowe, Brú na Bóinne and Bryn Celli Ddu.

Howler laughter, yes, sometimes with tears that cannot stop, disturbing across centuries and seas, like the keening of wolves when the traps have sprung. Laughter, at midwinter, that assures me of an armor, like tree bark when the sap is withdrawn, sighing, *Season, season, we all return with the season*. Root wisdom that says *I only laugh because you are tough, and I am this skin you wear*. Laughter so bright and bold, emphatic, that no words are needed to explain: *You will not be hung tonight, daughter, from the rafters of your children's, children's barns, and remaining chieftains are not destined for beheading, or a spectacle, for the entertainment of the perverse, of horses—unwilling—whipped, so as to rip bodies into pieces*. Having laid, in love and wild delight, for what? One night before this? One night of love amongst the rowan trees on that soft and dew-laden grass where hares roll and frolic under the fullness of a braw bricht nicht? Before the tyrant's men gun down whole families and rape who's left? With the *get* of your seed, father, with a mix of violence and defeat that only undoes sons, now and yet to be—a poison curse that cannot be reversed. 'Here, suck on the coffee,' I hear him echo from the corner of what I think of as a soul, 'and move closer to the hearth, they do not know this place, so you are as safe as ghosts and haunting poetry; my arms are your arms, *your babies also mine. This blanket was worn by my mother and she is you also, so just settle, kiddo.'*

Dear Father, I know who else you've been, life after life, garment after garment, because I have sat with your daughters—the mothers who bore me for forty generations—and the message is clear. Your message. A message that says: *I am the sleeping king, a sleeping beauty, yes. One day, upon a time, I will be woken by a terrible but liberating sword, and you'll understand just how beautiful I am; how beautiful you are. And history is the liar that says a briar of roses surrounds my slumbering fortress and that all who interweave, and inter-live within this impacted earth are whimsy, and a breath of confusion for children born into acceptance. But what have you done, daughter? How is it I am awoken?*

Father, it was a divide that brought us together. When you lost your love, and your children, to the cage and the banishment, her name dissolved, and those of the warrior and druid-trained, unkilled children, you knew, didn't you? Hers is the secret blood and sinew and portal. Father, I have lived to set us both free, even though the scattered stones on the shores of Medway, Ure, Thames and River Ribble, of Pegwell Bay still hold their breath at what was done...

> *The army then marched against the Silures, a naturally fierce people and now full of confidence in the might of Caractacus, who by many an indecisive and many a successful battle had raised himself far above all the other generals of the Britons. Inferior in military strength, but deriving an advantage from the deceptiveness of the country, he at once shifted the war by a stratagem into the territory of the Ordovices, where, joined by all who dreaded peace with us, he resolved on a final struggle.*
>
> —Tacitus, *Annals: Book Twelve*

...Of the hill watched by the mighty Menai.

They never included me, or my children, nor theirs either, and yet here we are! And Father, I have this to say: thank you. For the boar-spirit. For Mother deer and fox, and moaning slave. For all the countless owl eggs, hatched and discarded upon the forest floor. For the thorns that sing of roses, for the eagle pipes, and the bladder of cattle stitched tight to form an uilleann; reed chanter and drone—*an phìob mhòr,* the brothers from around Strathclyde call her—sounding just the same as the howl of dread, when the mine collapses, with only my uncles to emerge, altered for life, their seed, within the womb of my mother, remembering.

Father, I see it all: the muskets and the bombing over London. The ravens in the tower of the usurper, and the *mewl* of dead babies discarded in sewers and trenches and unmarked graves. I am my own mothers, in the terrible days and nights of plague, century on top of
century, who make it into the sunlight with me in their arms, a dirt-ground refugee in these lands that are us.

Dear Father, you are kinda dead, and for too many years I didn't understand the depths of the capacity for cruelty that human beings have at their hands, in paperwork and rubber stamps, from behind distant oak-stolen doors, from within the sweat of double chins, exclaiming sentences of abandonment and slavery from mothballed ermine collars, and powdered wigs, with a shotgun hidden in their folds of scarlet.

I didn't understand anything. Not one thing. Until I found you and realized the maps are right in front of these eyes. I rubbed the sleep from them even though my sight was blurred because of it. Dear, dearest father, all I saw was that fearsome tree of life and I never understood that he was you. Holding gravestones from their final fall in the long-forgotten churchyards of a careless and condescending religion.

I knew the knives. I took the poison. I vomited up herons and seals, hedgehogs and enormous, ragged bears, and when I wiped my mouth to remove the taste of their ruin you said, '*Hey! Take some more of that stuff into you, we're getting closer now.*'

I knew the smell of yesterday but how can a body recognize a scent except from within a body? That's how it is, you know, dear father, when the forests of this alien, ancient land that is not ours and never was, burns, the people-critters exploding from sap-filled eucalypts, or straining, inevitably and impossibly, to breathe from where they seek to shelter; the burrows and the hollows and the stripped down bark of ant and cicada trees. That smell is known by your body; which is every human body born through you. A sweet stink of fear. As much from the ballista as from lightning and campfire and hearth fire—*croi bhaile*.

It is autumn now. Here. We were conceived in autumn, father. This life, this body, you, all other fathers, all our mothers, all your daughters, all your now-dead sons. Father, I have a suitcase. It is filled with files, and almost none of them say your name. But magic and wit have a way, don't they? Or ducking when the beating is about to
begin. When the truncheons and the dungeons and whippings and isolation take out the louder, ones.

Father, you were never lost. My eyes were averted, the lie was forced upon me. But still, for all that, I am so, so sorry that I was not your witness. When the prison door slammed and you were wide-eyed in the stink of rat shit and the sweat of the terrified who laid, as you, upon the stone bench that the guards—mockingly—called a bed. When you starved to death, despite the metal tube, your excrement upon the walls in letters, made of English, that yelled HELP ME! before the hoses hit you with the violence of controlled, restrained and trained-in-attack, once free, now harvested-for-sadism-restyled water.

Father, how well you fucked the woman who would become a wily, hidden mother. How peculiar and awful a reality that your name has not died. How exquisite was the moment I learned of you; that I am made of the stuff and rot and starlight of heroes. This letter is a thing of alliance. Of recognition. Oh, of profound and hair-raising, blood-sap-rising pride.

Father, almost two thousand years have surrounded frost-filled mornings and nights of hangings and prayers, of ships drowning sisters, and children forced by strangers onto women who become your daughters and your sons. I know you know; I know you know, too.

And so, I pack my bundle. Of deer hide and unborn spruce, filled with me before I lie down beneath the broken branches, to be a boulder, or a Galloway, or a southern right whale, bones bleached and marked with runes and ogham, covered in moss, lichen-red and pale grey-green, I have this to tell you, father...

There is not an end in sight.
Your loving daughter,
And hers, and her sons
And theirs.
And theirs.

...

THE SONG OF LEVINGTON BLADE

(for those who fear)

Within the darkness one is waiting;
a child of life unborn, alone,
until the season of confusion
when the darkness turns to stone.

The one – the only covenant –
that life called from the crown
will call you when it's ready;
when its web is fully spun.

From the forest to the garden
to the desert to the tomb;
to the place of revolution
where no sun has ever shone.

Within the dance of death's embrace
the seed is carried past the veil.
It is unfolding to its pattern
and a forest is its grail.

The song – not yet – of what will be;
the child of life is forming
and you'll sing it with each other
when it's born within its morning.

From the forest to the garden
to the desert to the sea,
to the place of resolution
where the child will mother be;

and another and another
in an endless symphony.
The seed is just one season
to the seasons of the tree...
And the tree is of the forest
of the earth that's yet to be.

MUTHA

I place myself at the center of the table,
The position of power,
And sit on the seat that faces the potion of poison
And stare it down and remember
Worn down allegiances and dare them to farewell me
With platitudes at my funeral.
It's appropriate to raise an eyebrow
To be sour,
To glower at the presumption of fate
In which I seem doomed to this room,
To this hour—
To this isolated, tarted, tepid, feted, under-furnished
And over-rated hotel room with no adequate shower,
No room service, not at any hour.
I can leave if I want, that's not the point!
And I remember no home, no matter,
Fucking mad as the mad hatter,
and no one to plead to;
To read Jung into this need to be real, to feel, to heal.
No longer content to conceal the desire to devour the
Dross of dead things from Kennedy
and honest government,
to dogs, places and cats,
Propaganda called facts, the I love yous with
Other agendas behind their backs.
I'm an achiever, a believer, a no-needer
No need to please
So it sucks that I'm stuck with these uncountable
Specks of dust that once were innocences and trusts,
That I'm here and alone
With this jar of grey powder,
This poison, this wire,
This reason,
Aware of the glare of the neon that leaks

Flashing, electric flickering,
Illuminating the room. Hey!
It's cheery. Like Christmas! Now that's dust.
Drink the draught, fuck you, I tell myself,
And lie on the bed and re-read Towelhead
Till you're dead.
Then my mobile goes off. I've got a message
And it's urgent and to move it.
Someone I love is in trouble,
been bashed and is in the hospital
and the bubble bursts
and I pocket the poison along with my phone and
take up another position.
As mother.

Who gets it for this?
Here's the purpose for the poison.
Am I capable of murder?
Be The Crow and call it justice?
Sure.
I've carried this bottle of bullshit,
And added so much it's homeopathic
And just one mote
In the throat of the next fucking
Unjust hustler who busts up a kid of mine
Or somebody else I love gets it.
I say 'put the bunny back in the box',
Always accepting of an apology
But only from good company.

Then I'm there at the hospital
With my chin stuck out.
And I place myself at the centre of the situation,
The position of power,
The seat that faces the potion of poison
And I stare it down.

WOMAN MOUNTAIN

Here, again's the same song,
the towering, mountain name song
of tyranny and contentious, momentous and unearned gain:
of woman—the mountain—
who doesn't answer to claimed names because...
She tells this tale of shredded limbs and broken minds, violation; mothers' tears
and husk-like, crushed humanity that forgets just what it isn't—
A relic of eternity that only tells about ten thousand years
And transforms the people of forest and mountain and fjord and lake
into barbed wire and cement and some spent uranium's genome prison
Because of a nameless certain something that messages us
Daily,
of the relentlessness of being;
of a pizza, plastic, poison, pointless, confusing, screen-time neon way of seeing.

We want access to it all: the things your thighs hide, so open wide.
Hey! they chant in someone's language.
Hey witch! Hey god! Hey you! We're wearing white! We're here to pay you homage!
So cough it up—the precious-stuff; we demand this mountain's message,
not of frost or ice or snow or silence...but the way through, the passage.
The oil, where the gas is, the easy way to the wonderland of prestige,
Open up that fucking frozen road to the payload where the ice dies;
where the winter is no more.
We climbed here, just to let you know...
You better vomit up the good shit, the meaning of this mountain the whole shebang, the fucken show.

You're a rock, a destination, the place the hermits thought to grow to give life meaning without mercy.
You're supposed to be surrendered, and a summit, and we want something we can sell to make us famous,
So shut down the excuses, your words, your whining and your wildness...
You're a mountain that's a woman so you cannot, will not, shall not make us go!

She shrugs from being limestone, obsidian, basalt; quartz and gold, from being schist and gneiss, diamonds and coal, from being the patience of the lava, from being boulders, mammoth bones.
And first off, she says, *No comment—you still here? Who's your mummy then; your father, eh? Poor wee deaf, dumb, blind and clueless things of nameless, never-faced fear.*
What is it you were before this; is it true you once sang joyous, wanton; clear?
What happened in the maelstrom, that you despise the joy of peace? No? No answer?

Before she smiles some kind of violence

And whispers, oh so quietly, *well, you really had to ask,*
So hey, be righteous,
Take my backbone and my breast milk made of winter, and my endless broken hallways,
because you're gutless, and you're brain-fried, inside that manufactured mask.
But the birdwings made of nightmares are you, falling from this mountain, oh, so flightless,
to where you started, on that waiting cracking, hungry arctic glass.

She says—

I'm the bottomless, broken vessel that holds all your wounded men.
I have been here for eternity and will stay until the *when*

of my sons within their millions, hanging—mutilated, raging, burning—
because they chose to die, not bend... if they even had the choice to choose a thing.

I'm the space that's like night-shadow, between your stolen, pompous words
and the promise that will break them, and confront them, and confound them and command them,
Like they did with those Macdonald's, grassless, unloved herds...
That your breath is only lung rise, with a limit, before no more;
That when you taste the galling emptiness of every love song that absolutely wasn't
And your fingers lose their grip on the dinner table, the writing table, the foldout Sunday picnic table...
Bleed rivers of moss and drought and acid soil and whalebone onto the fable of the ghosts of slaughtered birds;
when they confront life's final door that never was and so still isn't
maybe then, in wind and susurration, pebble-rumble and avalanche
you'll hear the words

That

I sometimes open up to you
And take away your pain
But in the taking sometimes rend you empty
And messily insane.

So if you ask my purpose
Be very well prepared
for those who came before you
Saw only what they dared

And when I took them to an edge, said it's deeper than you wanted, eh?
They backed up, hid and lied and lied, until the others in white take

you away because
You wouldn't take the depths I haunted, or any wisdom I have offered.
So take your time and certain be, or fuck, I'll lay my gauntlet down...
And forever, then, unsparingly will you and everyone, and everything just drown.
You thought you could impress me with this shit show? Without counting on the slaughtered?
Never was, never could be the only circus in, on, bulldozing through ol' Mountain woman town;
Never gave you a pass, or prominence or position for the lie that you could cut my children down.

In knowing me you see yourself,
I'm your academic fear
So if you fluff those wings you stole from birds
Take very special care...
For you *will* turn to me when all is lost;
When you care no more to live
And you *will* gladly lose your sanity
If it was ever yours to give.
Because us mountains we are oceans we are tundra and we're moor
And you feed us, that's your purpose; I could have been quiet but you asked me for some door
And so...
Get off me—off this mountain—bow your forehead to the dirt upon some unburned cottage floor
Where carnage was once the clickbait and the gristle for the poor and...
And never say another thing, until you're very, very sure
That the song you sing is who you are; bring me THAT and maybe, in another thousand years
When I'm the bottom of some ocean and I can breathe again once more...

I'll forgive you.

SUGGESTED READING

Macfarlane, R.	Underland, Hamish Hamilton, 2019
	The Wild Places, Granta Books, 2007
	Landmarks, Random House, 2015
	Mountains of the Mins, Granta Books, 2003
	The Old Ways, Penguin Books, 2013
Monbiot, G.	Feral, Rewilding the Land, Sea and Human Life, Penguin Books, 2014
Crass, C.	Towards a Collective Liberation, PM Press, 2013
Cruden, L.	Walking the Maze, The Enduring Presence of the Celtic Spirit, Destiny, 1998
Berry, W.	World Ending Fire, Allen Lane, 2017
Kimmerer, R.	Braiding Sweetgrass, Milkweed, 2013
Kelly, L.	The Memory Code, Allen & Unwin, 2016
Saul, J. R.	Voltaire's Bastards, Simon & Schuster, 2013
	The Unconscious Civilization, Free Press, 1999
Scott, K.	Taboo, Pan Macmillan, 2017
Shaw, M.	A Branch from the Lightning Tree, White Cloud press, 2015

NOTES FROM UNDHR (unratified)

Article 1.

All human beings are born free and equal in dignity and rights. They are endowed with reason and conscience and should act towards one another in a spirit of brotherhood.

Article 2.
Everyone is entitled to all the rights and freedoms set forth in this Declaration, without distinction of any kind, such as race, colour, sex, language, religion, political or other opinion, national or social origin, property, birth or other status. Furthermore, no distinction shall be made on the basis of the political, jurisdictional or international status of the country or territory to which a person belongs, whether it be independent, trust, non-self-governing or under any other limitation of sovereignty.

Article 3.
Everyone has the right to life, liberty and security of person.

Article 4.
No one shall be held in slavery or servitude; slavery and the slave trade shall be prohibited in all their forms.

Article 5.
No one shall be subjected to torture or to cruel, inhuman or degrading treatment or punishment.

ABOUT LORE DE ANGELES

(1951 C.E. (whatever that means) —?)

LORE is the name chosen, upon being released from slavery at the age of 69 years old, as not so much a name as a function. De Angeles was trafficked, as an infant, and experienced deplorable and untold abuse at the hands of the strangers, to whom she was sold, privately and for a lot of money, in the months following her birth.

As a result of the apology, in 2013, by then Prime Minister of Australia Julia Gillard, de Angeles was able to set in place the process of her official recognition by both parents. She was aided in this by Ms Katrina Grace Kelly of CRIBMATES, and others mentioned in the acknowledgments, towards the beginning of this book.

Unfortunately, at the time of her freedom through an Australian Supreme Court, both parents were dead. De Angeles, with the help of her colleague at www.thesignsofthetimes.com.au has, however, traced her cultural lineage. She is able, now, to provide a true and unbiased accounting to her children, and theirs.

De Angeles lives with a form of synaesthesia. She sees words as literal. She is, therefore, extremely careful, not only of what she says, but also what she reads and hears, as all trigger responses not always meant by others. She considers this anomaly to be three things: normal, a gift and a curse.

De Angeles lives with what is termed *high functioning, lifetime, complex PTSD* and is, as such, what could be thought as an overachiever. A title de Angeles considers an impossibility.

Image 2021

ENDNOTES

[i] FROM THE DARLING DOWNS TO DON DALE: A LITANY OF MONSTROUS ACTS AGAINST INDIGENOUS CHILDREN, Paul Daley, The Guardian News, 2016: https://www.theguardian.com/commentisfree/2016/jul/30/from-the-darling-downs-to-don-dale-a-litany-of-monstrous-acts-against-indigenous-children

[ii] ENDA KENNY DESCRIBES TUAM BURIAL SITE AS A 'CHAMBER OF HORRORS: The Journal, Ireland:
https://www.thejournal.ie/leaders-questions-30-3275086-Mar2017/

[iii] DR. PAUL SUNDERLAND, ADOPTION AND ADDICTION, REMEMBERED NOT RECALLED: https://adopteeidentityrites.com/2014/09/04/adoption-and-addiction-remembered-not-recalled/

[iv] UN SLAVERY ABOLITION DAY:
https://www.un.org/en/observances/slavery-abolition-day